GREAT DISASTERS

FLOODS

FLOODS

Other books in the Great Disasters series:

GREAT DISASTERS

FLOODS

Nancy Harris, *Book Editor*

Daniel Leone, *President*
Bonnie Szumski, *Publisher*
Scott Barbour, *Managing Editor*

GREENHAVEN
PRESS®

San Diego • Detroit • New York • San Francisco • Cleveland
New Haven, Conn. • Waterville, Maine • London • Munich

For more information, contact
Greenhaven Press
27500 Drake Rd.
Farmington Hills, MI 48331-3535
Or you can visit our Internet site at http://www.gale.com

LIBRARY OF CONGRESS CATALOGING-IN-PUBLICATION DATA

Floods / Nancy Harris, book editor.
   p. cm. — (Great disasters)
  Includes bibliographical references and index.
  ISBN 0-7377-1878-1 (lib. bdg. : alk. paper) —
  ISBN 0-7377-1879-X (pbk. : alk. paper)
    1. Floods. 2. Floods—United States. I. Harris, Nancy. II. Great disasters
(Greenhaven Press)
  GB1399.F588 2003
  904'.5—dc21
                                        2003049018

CONTENTS

tory. Over two thousand people were killed in nearby Johnstown.

tionally accurate forecasts, the death toll and damages from the floods were kept to a minimum.

H umans have an ambivalent relationship with their home planet, nurtured on the one hand by Earth's bounty but devastated on the other hand by its catastrophic natural disasters. While these events are the results of the natural processes of Earth, their consequences for humans frequently include the disastrous destruction of lives and property. For example, when the volcanic island of Krakatau exploded in 1883, the eruption generated vast seismic sea waves called tsunamis that killed about thirty-six thousand people in Indonesia. In a single twenty-four-hour period in the United States in 1974, at least 148 tornadoes carved paths of death and destruction across thirteen states. In 1976, an earthquake completely destroyed the industrial city of Tangshan, China, killing more than 250,000 residents.

Some natural disasters have gone beyond relatively localized destruction to completely alter the course of human history. Archaeological evidence suggests that one of the greatest natural disasters in world history happened in A.D. 535, when an Indonesian "supervolcano" exploded near the same site where Krakatau arose later. The dust and debris from this gigantic eruption blocked the light and heat of the sun for eighteen months, radically altering weather patterns around the world and causing crop failure in Asia and the Middle East. Rodent populations increased with the weather changes, causing an epidemic of bubonic plague that decimated entire populations in Africa and Europe. The most powerful volcanic eruption in recorded human history also happened in Indonesia. When the volcano Tambora erupted in 1815, it ejected an estimated 1.7 million tons of debris in an explosion that was heard more than a thousand miles away and that continued to rumble for three months. Atmospheric dust from the eruption blocked much of the sun's heat, producing what was called "the year without summer" and creating worldwide climatic havoc, starvation, and disease.

As these examples illustrate, natural disasters can have as much impact on human societies as the bloodiest wars and most chaotic political revolutions. Therefore, they are as worthy of study as the major events of world history. As with the study of social and political events, the exploration of natural disasters can illuminate the causes of these catastrophes and target the lessons learned about how to mitigate and prevent the loss of life when disaster strikes again. By examining these events and the forces behind them, the Greenhaven Press Great Disasters series is designed to help students better understand such cataclysmic events. Each anthology in the series focuses on a specific type of natural disaster or a particular disastrous event in history. An introductory essay provides a general overview of the subject of the anthology, placing natural disasters in historical and scientific context. The essays that follow, written by specialists in the field, researchers, journalists, witnesses, and scientists, explore the science and nature of natural disasters, describing particular disasters in detail and discussing related issues, such as predicting, averting, or managing disasters. To aid the reader in choosing appropriate material, each essay is preceded by a concise summary of its content and biographical information about its author.

In addition, each volume contains extensive material to help the student researcher. An annotated table of contents and a comprehensive index help readers quickly locate particular subjects of interest. To guide students in further research, each volume features an extensive bibliography including books, periodicals, and related Internet websites. Finally, appendixes provide glossaries of terms, tables of measurements, chronological charts of major disasters, and related materials. With its many useful features, the Greenhaven Press Great Disasters series offers students a fascinating and awe-inspiring look at the deadly power of Earth's natural forces and their catastrophic impact on humans.

INTRODUCTION

When warlords began fighting in China around 400 B.C., the Yellow River began to be used as a combat weapon. Dikes along the river were often deliberately breached during the rainy season to flood enemy territory. The practice of using the river as a weapon of war continued until June 1938, when a Chinese general ordered his troops to dismantle a main dike to flood an advancing Japanese army during Japan's invasion of China at the beginning of World War II. The tactic worked, but much to the general's surprise and dismay, the break in the Yellow River's dike allowed the bulk of the river to flood more than nine thousand square miles, drowning an estimated five hundred thousand Chinese and leaving 6 million homeless. The area remained flooded for seven years.

Using a river as a combat weapon is unique, but people have been exploiting rivers for better or ill since they have inhabited the earth. Rivers were natural places to settle near because they supplied fresh drinking water, fish to eat, water to irrigate crops, and channels for shipping goods. Moreover, when rivers flooded during the rainy season, they deposited silt across farmers' fields, making the soil rich for crops. However, as the centuries advanced, people began to control rivers by building levees to prevent flooding and dams to control the flow of the waters. With the rivers seemingly under control, people felt safe and moved into the low-lying fertile regions bordering them. Unfortunately, like the Chinese general who discovered too late the folly of depending on a river to behave predictably, modern people living near "controlled" rivers have often found rivers uncooperative, unpredictable, even deadly. During periods of heavy rains, levees breach and dams disintegrate, freeing the river, whose waters engulf crops and homes, taking back the original floodplain.

"The Great Flood of '93" is a good example of these dynamics at work. In the summer of 1993 the Mississippi and Missouri Rivers overflowed their banks when summer rains, which would normally have swept through the Midwest and then vanished, were stalled for weeks in the area. These storms brought record-breaking rainfall. Rivers and their tributaries overflowed, prompting then-president Bill Clinton to declare major disasters in parts of nine states. An estimated fifty people were killed, seventy-two thousand homes were affected, and more than $10 billion in crop and property damage was reported. One of the reasons the damage was so extensive was that the river system had been altered over the previous century. Wetlands had been drained and then developed, and levees were built to protect people's property. In 1993, unfortunately, the swollen rivers breached these levees one by one. The greatest economic losses from the 1993 flood occurred in cities located on floodplains. In addition, the conversion of natural lands into farmlands resulted in high levels of runoff, which exaggerated the effects of the flooding; floodwaters eventually submerged 8 million acres of farmland.

The Great Flood of '93 illustrates the devastating power of floods, the most destructive of all natural disasters. A study between 1947 and 1967 found that at least 173,170 persons had died during that period as a direct result of riverine floods. Floods leave tens of thousands homeless, create famines due to the destruction of livestock and crops, and kill thousands from diseases such as cholera and typhoid that are caused by contaminated floodwaters. Because power lines may be broken and gas mains ruptured, major floods may also generate fires. Every year in the United States, floods cause an average of one hundred deaths and $2 billion in damages. In the late nineteenth and early twentieth centuries, river floods in China killed several million people, and in Bangladesh, where rivers regularly overflow their banks, thousands have been killed.

Flooding can be defined as any body of water overflowing into areas that are usually dry. Floods can occur near any stream or river on the earth under certain conditions. There are freshwater floods and floods caused by inundation from the sea. Flash floods are one of the most unpredictable and devastating of freshwater floods. These floods are caused by local torrential rains of short duration, usually six hours or less, as well as by dam breaks or the sudden breakup of winter ice jams in rivers. Although they are most common in the mountain and desert regions of the western United States, flash floods can occur almost anywhere. Other riverine floods are caused by heavy precipitation over large areas, which lasts from a few hours to several days. Sea floods are caused by storms striking at times of high tides, causing water to move inland. Some of the most devastating sea floods are caused when hurricane and cyclone winds stir up huge waves, which flood coastlines.

Most floods are naturally occurring events that distribute rich soils over the land and supply minerals and nutrients to the oceans. However, today flooding is becoming more prevalent and destructive due to human activities. Now the most destructive floods occur in heavily developed areas near rivers that have been "controlled" with levees and dams. Statistics show that record-breaking floods occurred along the Mississippi River in 1993 and 1995, along the Rhine in western Europe in December 1993 and January 1995, along the Yangtze in China in 1995 and 1998, and along the Elbe and Oder Rivers in central Europe during July 1997.

Although scientists believe that some of this flooding is a consequence of global warming, which would increase temperatures and might lead to heavier rainfall, many believe that the serious floods of the twentieth century are simply due to the fact that humankind has changed the hydrology of many river basins by building dams and levees and reducing the extent of floodplains. As populations grow in floodplains, covering normally absorbent land with concrete and buildings, floodwater runoff is accelerated, creating flood problems for communities. These problems are aggravated by the traditional practice of controlling floods with dams and levees. Dams and levees break and continually need to be repaired and maintained. Dam failures can cause huge floods. Levees, which channel water from one area to another, often protect people upstream from floods at the expense of those downstream, who are often on the receiving end of floodwaters.

Although some government agencies still support the use of dams and levees, as well as development in floodplains, others are encouraging the deconstruction of dams and levees, where possible, and discouraging further floodplain development. These new approaches, they believe, will help reduce deaths from floods, save billions of dollars spent on rebuilding in areas that are repeatedly flooded, and allow the floodplains to return to their natural state. Restoring floodplains would also help natural wetlands rebound. These areas, which include swamps and marshes, can store excess water like a sponge, alleviating flooding by providing natural areas into which rivers can overflow.

The more flooding that occurs as a result of human activities, the more it is necessary for scientists to develop sophisticated flood forecasting and prevention to prevent, or at least minimize, the destructiveness of floods. The U.S. National Weather Service monitors rivers with thirteen high-tech river forecast centers. At each center a team of meteorologists, hydrologists, water management experts, and hydraulic engineers charts all water movement to forecast when and how much rivers might rise. The scientists receive a constant stream of data from automated rain gauges, measuring stations in rivers and streams, satellite pictures, and Doppler radar. They then feed this data into computer models, which analyze it. Hydrologists use the resulting analysis, combined with their personal experience and common sense, to improve flood forecasting. Despite constant vigilance and advances in forecasting methods, however, flood forecasting is an inexact science. Although a flood is a relatively simple phenomenon, it presents complex problems to scientists. Even the most sophisticated computers cannot solve the theoretical engineering problems presented by flooding, which involve dams, levees, soil characteristics, and rainfall. In consequence, many scientists believe prevention, not forecasting, is the best approach to mitigating flood damage.

As long as humans continue to live and work alongside rivers, disastrous floods like the Great Flood of '93 are likely to occur. However, as scientists learn more about the human causes of floods, they are developing new ideas about how to get the most advantage from rivers without destroying natural systems that help keep disastrous floods to a minimum. For, as the Chinese army general discovered the hard way, rivers, as important as they are to human life, can be deadly.

The Science and Study of Floods

About Floods and Flood Designations

PART 1 BY JOE A. MORELAND; PART 2 BY KAREN DINICOLA

Floods are common disasters, responsible for one hundred deaths and $2 billion in damages a year in the United States. In Part 1 of this selection, Joe A. Moreland, a hydrologist at the United States Geological Survey (USGS), explains that floods are usually caused by intense storms, which produce so much rain that an area or stream cannot hold all the water. Rivers can also flood when snow melts, dams fail, or when ice jams or landslides block river channels, according to Moreland. Normally dry land can be flooded by high lake levels, high tides, or by waves blown inland by hurricanes or cyclones. The hydrologist further explains that floods can occur anytime, but by observing weather patterns, scientists can determine when and where floods will probably occur. In Part 2 of this selection, USGS hydrologist Karen Dinicola writes that hydrologists study the flow records of streams over a minimim of ten years, collecting data to detemine the possible size of floods and their probable occurrence rate. According to Dinicola, government agencies have mapped areas of past flooding and estimated that a person living in a floodplain has a one in two chance of experiencing a flood in his or her lifetime.

Part 1
Floods Are Common and Costly Natural Disasters

When rivers overflow their banks, or flood, they can cause damage to property and crops. Floods are common and costly natural disasters. In the United States, the average annual cost of flood damage is more than $2 billion.

Joe A. Moreland, "Floods and Flood Plains," *USGS Fact Sheet OFR 93-641*, August 2001. Karen Dinicola, "The '100-Year Flood,'" *USGS Fact Sheet FS 229-96*, April 2002.

Each year about 100 people lose their lives to floods.
Floods usually are local, short-lived events that can happen
suddenly, sometimes with little or no warning. They usually are
caused by intense storms that produce more runoff than an area
can store or a stream can carry within its normal channel. Rivers
can also flood when dams fail, when ice jams or landslides temporarily block a channel, or when snow melts rapidly. In a
broader sense, normally dry lands can be flooded by high lake
levels, by high tides, or by waves driven ashore by strong winds.
Small streams, particularly in the Southwest, are subject to flash
floods (very rapid increases in runoff), which may last from a few
minutes to a few hours. On larger streams, floods usually last from
several hours to a few days. A series of storms might keep a river
above flood stage (the water level at which a river overflows its
banks) for several weeks.

Weather Patterns Can Determine When Floods Occur

Floods can occur at any time, but weather patterns have a strong
influence on when and where floods happen. Cyclones, or storms
that bring moisture inland from the ocean, can cause floods in
the winter and early spring in the western United States. Thunderstorms are relatively small but intense storms that can cause
flash floods in smaller streams in late summer and fall in the
Southwest. Frontal storms form at the front of large, moist air
masses moving across the country and can cause floods in the
northern and eastern parts of the United States during the winter and spring. Hurricanes are intense tropical storms that can
cause floods in the Southeast during the late summer and fall.

Making Flood Designations

The size, or magnitude, of a flood is described by a term called
recurrence interval. By studying a long period of flow records for
a stream, it is possible to estimate the size of a flood that would,
for example, have a 5-year recurrence interval (called a 5-year
flood). A year flood is one that would occur, on the average, once
every five years. . . .

Flood Plains Normally Are Dry

Flood plains are lands bordering rivers and streams that normally
are dry but are covered with water during floods. Buildings or

other structures placed in flood plains can be damaged by floods. They also can change the pattern of water flow and increase flooding and flood damage on adjacent property by blocking the flow of water and increasing the width, depth, or velocity of flood waters.

Flood-plain zoning, which places restrictions on the use of land on flood plains, can reduce the cost of flood damage. Local governments may pass laws that prevent uncontrolled building or development on flood plains to limit flood risks and to protect nearby property. Landowners in areas that adopt local ordinances or laws to limit development on flood plains can purchase flood insurance to help cover the cost of damage from floods.

Dams and Levees Can Reduce the Risk of Floods

Flood-control dams have been built on many streams and rivers to store storm runoff and reduce flooding downstream. Although the same volume of water must eventually move down the river, the peak flow (the largest rate of streamflow during a flood) can be reduced by temporarily storing water and releasing it when river levels have fallen. Levees are artificial river banks built to control the spread of flood waters and to limit the amount of land covered by floods. Levees provide protection from some floods but can be over-topped or eroded away by large floods. For example, levees failed to protect vast areas in the Mississippi and Missouri River valleys during the record-setting floods that occurred in 1993.

Part 2

The term "100-year flood" is misleading because it leads people to believe that it happens only once every 100 years. The truth is that an uncommonly big flood can happen any year. The term "100-year flood" is really a statistical designation, and there is a *1-in-100 chance* that a flood this size will happen during any year. Perhaps a better term would be the "1-in-100 chance flood."

The actual number of years between floods of any given size varies a lot. Big floods happen irregularly because the climate naturally varies over many years. We sometimes get big floods in successive or nearly successive years with several very wet years in a row.

How Floods Are Designated

Scientists collect data and study past floods to get a minimum of 10 years of information about the river; a longer record provides a better estimate of the "1-in-100 chance flood." Scientists use statistics and observe how frequently different sizes of floods occurred, and the average number of years between them, to determine the probability that a flood of any given size will be equaled or exceeded during any year.

As more data are collected, or when a river basin is altered in a way that affects the flow of water in the river, scientists re-evaluate the frequency of flooding. Dams and urban development are examples of some man-made changes in a basin that affect floods.

Scientists at the USGS [United States Geological Survey] measure streamflow in rivers across the State during every major flood. After flood waters recede, the USGS may be funded to locate and survey "high-water marks" where debris and mud lines indicate the highest extent of flood waters. These post-flood surveys are used to estimate maximum flows at sites that could not be reached during the floods and also to map the areas covered by the floods.

Mapping the Floodplains

The areas affected by past floods have been mapped by the Federal Emergency Management Agency and many other government agencies. Because of continuing changes in river channels and land use in many basins, the maps may not reflect current information for your area. If you live on the designated floodplain, the chances are about 1 in 2 that you will experience a flood during your lifetime.

Floods Will Continue to Happen

Although we can lessen effects of some floods, they are part of the natural cycle of every river and benefit instream habitats by moving material downstream and renewing streambeds. As floods get bigger and spread farther, flood waters slow and deposit sediment on the floodplain. This natural process created valuable farmlands in river valleys of the Pacific Northwest over thousands of years.

Types of Floods

By Charles A. Perry

Floods are defined as the accumulation of too much water in too little time in a specific area. According to Charles A. Perry, a research hydrologist for the United States Geological Survey (USGS), floods were the number one natural disaster in the twentieth century in terms of lost lives and property damage. In this selection, Perry explains that there are different types of floods. Regional floods are caused by extended periods of rainfall, which saturate the ground; because the ground is saturated, any additional rain runs off into streams and rivers, which eventually overflow their banks and cause flooding. Flash floods, deadly floods that occur in a matter of seconds or hours, produce rapidly rising water levels that flow with incredible velocity. Perry also describes ice-jam, storm-surge, and dam- and levee-failure floods as well as floods caused by landslides and volcanic mudflows.

During the 20th century, floods were the number-one natural disaster in the United States in terms of number of lives lost and property damage. They can occur at any time of the year, in any part of the country, and at any time of the day or night. Most lives are lost when people are swept away by flood currents, whereas most property damage results from inundation by sediment-laden water. Flood currents also possess tremendous destructive power, as lateral forces can demolish buildings and erosion can undermine bridge foundations and footings leading to the collapse of structures. . . .

Floods are the result of a multitude of naturally occurring and human-induced factors, but they all can be defined as the accumulation of too much water in too little time in a specific area. Types of floods include regional floods, flash floods, ice-jam floods, storm-surge floods, dam- and levee-failure floods, and debris, landslide, and mudflow floods.

Charles A. Perry, "Significant Floods in the United States During the 20th Century—USGS Measures a Century of Floods," *USGS Fact Sheet 024-00*, March 2000.

Types of Floods

Regional Floods. Some regional floods occur seasonally when winter or spring rains coupled with melting snow fill river basins with too much water too quickly. The ground may be frozen, reducing infiltration into the soil and thereby increasing runoff. Such was the case for the New England flood of March 1936 in which more than 150 lives were lost and property damage totaled $300 million.

Extended wet periods during any part of the year can create saturated soil conditions, after which any additional rain runs off into streams and rivers, until river capacities are exceeded. Regional floods are many times associated with slow-moving, low-pressure or frontal storm systems including decaying hurricanes or tropical storms. Persistent wet meteorological patterns are usually responsible for very large regional floods such as the Mississippi River Basin flood of 1993 wherein damages were $20 billion.

Flash Floods. Flash floods can occur within several seconds to several hours, with little warning. Flash floods can be deadly because they produce rapid rises in water levels and have devastating flow velocities.

Several factors can contribute to flash flooding. Among these are rainfall intensity, rainfall duration, surface conditions, and topography and slope of the receiving basin. Urban areas are susceptible to flash floods because a high percentage of the surface area is composed of impervious streets, roofs, and parking lots where runoff occurs very rapidly. Mountainous areas also are susceptible to flash floods, as steep topography may funnel runoff into a narrow canyon. Floodwaters accelerated by steep stream slopes can cause the floodwave to move downstream too fast to allow escape, resulting in many deaths. A flash flood caused by 15 inches of rain in 5 hours from slow-moving thunderstorms killed 237 people in Rapid City, South Dakota, in 1972.

Floodwaves more than 30-feet high have occurred many miles from the rainfall area, catching people unaware. Even desert arroyos are not immune to flash floods, as distant thunderstorms can produce rapid rises in water levels in otherwise dry channels. Early-warning gages upstream save lives by providing advanced notice of potential deadly floodwaves.

Ice-Jam Floods. Ice-jam floods occur on rivers that are totally or partially frozen. A rise in stream stage will break up a totally

Flash floods occur without much warning, and can be extremely powerful. These cars were carried downstream by the force of a flash flood.

frozen river and create ice flows that can pile up on channel obstructions such as shallow riffles, log jams, or bridge piers. The jammed ice creates a dam across the channel over which the water and ice mixture continues to flow, allowing for more jamming to occur. Backwater upstream from the ice dam can rise rapidly and overflow the channel banks. Flooding moves downstream when the ice dam fails, and the water stored behind the dam is released. At this time the flood takes on the characteristics of a flash flood, with the added danger of ice flows that, when driven by the energy of the floodwave, can inflict serious damage on structures. An added danger of being caught in an ice-jam flood is hypothermia, which can quickly kill. Ice jams on the Yukon River in Alaska contributed to severe flooding during the spring breakup of 1992.

Storm-Surge Floods. Storm-surge flooding is water that is pushed up onto otherwise dry land by onshore winds. Friction between the water and the moving air creates drag that, depending upon the distance of water (fetch) and the velocity of the wind, can pile water up to depths greater than 20 feet. Intense, low-pressure systems and hurricanes can create storm-surge flooding. The storm surge is unquestionably the most dangerous part of a hurricane as pounding waves create very hazardous flood currents. Nine out of 10 hurricane fatalities are caused by the storm surge. Worst-case scenarios occur when the storm surge occurs concurrently with high tide. Stream flooding is much worse inland during the storm surge because of backwater effects. In September 1900, the hurricane and storm surge at Galveston, Texas, killed more than 6,000 people, making it the worst natural disaster in the Nation's history.

Dam- and Levee-Failure Floods. Dams and levees are built for flood protection. They usually are engineered to withstand a flood with a computed risk of occurrence. For example, a dam or levee may be designed to contain a flood at a location on a stream that has a certain probability of occurring in any 1 year. If a larger flood occurs, then that structure will be overtopped. If during the overtopping the dam or levee fails or is washed out, the water behind it is released to become a flash flood. Failed dams or levees can create floods that are catastrophic to life and property because of the tremendous energy of the released water. Warnings of the Teton Dam failure in Idaho in June 1976 reduced the loss of life to 11 people.

Debris, Landslide, and Mudflow Floods. Debris or landslide floods are created by the accumulation of debris, mud, rocks, and (or) logs in a channel, which form a temporary dam. Flooding occurs upstream as water becomes stored behind the temporary dam and then becomes a flash flood as the dam is breached and rapidly washes away. Landslides can create large waves on lakes or embayments and can be deadly. Mudflow floods can occur when volcanic activity rapidly melts mountain snow and glaciers, and the water mixed with mud and debris moves rapidly downslope. These mudflow events are also called lahars and, after the eruption of Mt. St. Helens in 1980, caused significant damage downstream along the Toutle and Cowlitz Rivers in southwest Washington. . . .

Flood Facts
- Most flood-related deaths are due to flash floods.
- Fifty percent of all flash-flood fatalities are vehicle related.
- Ninety percent of those who die in hurricanes drown.
- Most homeowners' insurance policies do not cover floodwater damage.

The Study of Flash Floods

By Robert Henson

Flash floods are responsible for the deaths of about one hundred Americans a year, making them among the deadliest of weather hazards. In this selection, Robert Henson explains that flash floods are caused by heavy storms that stall out over a particular area or by many storms passing the same area in a period of about six hours or less. Henson reports that forecasters have made advances in flash flood predictions with the help of computer models, but such models are incapable of predicting smallest-scale flash floods and floods caused by levee and dam failures.

Robert Henson is a writer, photographer, and meteorologist. He is a contributing editor of Weatherwise *magazine and a frequent writer for* The Weather Notebook, *a national radio program sponsored by the Mt. Washington Observatory. Henson is also a writer and editor at the National Center for Atmospheric Research and author of the book* The Rough Guide to Weather.

Rapid Creek sounded like a freight train passing in the night. "We could hear people trapped on houses on the other side of the creek crying . . . for help," remembered Jerry Mashek, an editor from the *Rapid City/South Dakota Journal* sent to cover the devastating June 1972 flood. "It was pitch black, rain was falling in sheets, and all we could do was listen to their pleas. How many people were swept to their deaths in that area alone, I'll never know. I could only feel helplessness and try not to hear the trapped people."

Derik Emery, a survivor of the flood, recalled the horror of watching people swept along on raging waters to their death. He had escaped by climbing onto a shed just before the flood hit.

Robert Henson, "In a Flash!" *Weatherwise*, vol. 50, August/September 1997, p. 30. Copyright © 1997 by Helen Dwight Reid Educational Foundation. Reproduced by permission. Published by Heldref Publications, 1319 18th Street, NW, Washington, DC 20036-1802.

"We saw one man sitting on a house trailer, riding it on the water down the ravine at 30 or 40 miles an hour. We never saw him again." The floodwaters also washed away three children from a neighboring trailer. "That's the worst thing there is . . . when you see people screaming for help and you can't do anything about it . . . especially the kids."

Another survivor, with tears coming to his eyes, remembered seeing a couple clinging to the top of a camper in the high water, screaming "Help us!! Help us!!" "There was nothing we could do," said the man.

In all, the Rapid City flood of June 9, 1972, killed 237 people, one of the deadliest flooding disasters in U.S. history. Several other major flash floods occurred in the 1970s, the nation's worst decade for flash floods. Today, flash floods kill about 100 Americans each year, keeping them among the deadliest of weather hazards. This is half of the annual death toll in the 1970s, but many more than the yearly total in the 1940s and 1950s.

Improvements in prediction, detection, and warning since the 1970s have paid off, as no single U.S. flood has killed more than 100 people since 1980. With the help of computer models, better radars and rain gauges, and other tools, forecasters can now spot prototypical flash floods as they form and get the word out to the public in time.

However, the war is far from won. Like a mutating virus, the flash-flood threat is taking on new dimensions that can stymie the most sophisticated forecast and warning efforts. Growing urban areas play havoc with local hydrology, making thousands of motorists vulnerable to quickly rising streams and creeks. And the nation's aging network of flood-control structures is showing its frailty, with large-scale floods turning into flash floods as dams and levees give way.

The "Flash" in Flood

Flash floods are defined as those that play out over a few hours, usually six or less. (More leisurely "river flooding" takes days or weeks to unfold.) Typically, flash floods occur when several hours of extremely heavy rainfall deluges small river basins far beyond capacity. However, a longer-term bout of heavy rain can also indirectly trigger a flash flood by straining levees until they fail.

Unlike most other weather threats, flash floods spring directly from the nature of a landscape and its human alterations. For these reasons, flash-flood forecasting is a hybrid art, calling for knowledge of hydrology and topography as well as meteorology. Computer simulations can blend each of these elements for guidance, but a good forecaster needs to know about how floods happen in order to make best use of the computer's help. Just as important is a cool head. Flash floods often occur in tandem with tornadoes, hurricanes, and other kinds of extreme weather, which puts added stress on those with warning responsibility. "We have a lot of evidence that the really big events, like the Madison County, Virginia, flood [a near-catastrophe in June 1995] are being better forecast," says Matt Kelsch, who instructs National Weather Service (NWS) staff at a hydrometeorology course held at the University Corporation for Atmospheric Research in Boulder, Colorado. "On the other hand, the smaller events that are occurring in conjunction with severe weather are slipping through the cracks."

"People may not be dying a hundred at a time, but they're dying 11 at a time," says Eve Gruntfest, a geographer at the University of Colorado at Colorado Springs. This scattering of mini-disasters, according to Gruntfest, makes it harder to tell when safety measures are working. "If a flood happens and 11 people die, was the warning a success?"

Issuing Flash Flood Warnings

On the evening of May 5, 1995, a slow-moving storm complex bombarded the Dallas–Fort Worth area. An outdoor festival near Fort Worth [Texas] had only a few minutes' warning before baseball-sized hail pelted thousands of patrons. Severe thunderstorm and tornado warnings went up, but the worst threat was yet to materialize. A faster-moving squall line overtook the initial supercell near Dallas [Texas], and a huge swath of moist air was lifted above the city, squeezing out rainfall at the rate of up to nine inches an hour. "This sort of thing probably happens fairly often," says Kelsch, "but not usually over a big city."

According to Kelsch, "Despite being overwhelmed by severe weather, the NWS got out a flash-flood warning minutes before the first fatality occurred, while there was still a tornado warning in effect." By night's end, 15 people had died in flooding, while lightning had killed three more. A similar event occurred in Cheyenne, Wyoming, on August 1, 1985, when a flash-flood warning was issued just after a tornado warning expired, leaving some residents unsure whether to seek low or high ground. One woman drowned in her basement.

Boxcars and Backbuilding

How can forecasters anticipate a flash flood? By their very nature, they are highly local events, often impossible to pinpoint far in advance. However, meteorologists are now able to spot the large-scale patterns that could yield an extreme rainfall somewhere in a forecast region within 12 to 24 hours. Although a strong mid-level jet stream is a key ingredient for tornado-producing thunderstorms, it actually works against extreme flooding. The jet tends to move showers and thunderstorms along at a good clip, thus reducing the odds of extended rainfall at any one spot.

What's needed for a flash flood is a setup where heavy storms either linger over one spot for hours, or else move and regenerate in such a way that cell after cell passes over the same spot. The latter radar signature is called "training" or a "train echo," with each

Flash floods are one of the deadliest weather hazards, and frequently result in the loss of life. Here, rescuers fight a strong current as they drag a man back to safety.

cell analogous to a boxcar that passes over the same track as its predecessors. The analogy isn't perfect: the meteorological train tends to shift to one side with time, eventually bringing an end to the heavy rain. Even worse than training echoes is backbuilding, where a storm develops on its back edge as quickly as it moves forward. "In backbuilding, you don't get a break at all," says Kelsch. If winds are weak at all levels, a storm complex will eventually choke on its own rain cooled air and dissipate. A steady source of fuel is required to ensure the health of a slow-moving, flood-producing storm. That source is typically a low-level stream of warm, moist air, which may be moving into the cell from below at a faster clip than the mid-level winds above.

Mountains are an ideal place for this scenario to unfold. In the 1976 Big Thompson Canyon flood in Colorado, stiff moist easterly winds blew from the plains into the narrow canyon, where they were forced upward. Weak higher-level winds blew from the southeast. The resulting storm elements moved northwest as the complex slowly drifted east, keeping the same areas under rain for hours. Another common scenario is for a stationary front to align itself parallel to a weak mid-level jet stream, allowing storms to form along the front, move slowly to the front's cool side, then regenerate along the front.

No matter how they develop, flood-producing storms can't be stingy with their output. Only part of the water vapor that ascends into a storm falls out as rain or hail. The rest evaporates or forms clouds. As one might expect, the more moist an air mass, the better the likelihood of flooding. "The cloud droplets in these moist conditions tend to be smaller but packed more densely then they are in other storms," says Kelsch. A new kind of Doppler radar may soon help the NWS gauge the size and shape of droplets in a particular storm and whether it is more prone to yield hail or heavy rain.

Ground Zero

Sometimes what's happening at ground level can make the difference between a garden-variety downpour and a serious flash flood. The weather situation on July 12, 1996, wasn't a classic one for flooding in Colorado. Severe storms with heavy rain were predicted, but a mid-level jet blowing at 60 m.p.h. was forecast to keep the storms moving quickly enough to limit the flood potential.

However, a forest fire two months earlier made all the difference. The May 19 fire had stripped bare a hillside near Buffalo Creek, about 25 miles southwest of Denver. Trees and shrubs that normally absorb or impede runoff were gone. Moreover, the resins and oils on the ground from the burned pine trees were hydrophobic, or water-repellent, allowing runoff to cascade down the land surface "almost as if it were a parking lot," says Kelsch. The result was a small but severe flash flood along Buffalo Creek that killed two people.

Along with land features like fire scars, many other variables affect flood potential, such as the heights of rivers and creeks and the amount of moisture in the soil. Many of these factors can be accounted for in computer models that simulate how a given rainfall in a given time period will flow into river basins and what kind of flood might result. Here, weather forecasters rely on colleagues at the NWS River Forecast Centers (RFCs) to provide large-scale guidance.

A Leading Computer Model

One of the leading computer models was created at the Sacramento [California] RFC, where Eric Strem is development and operations hydrologist. "Given the current soil moisture conditions and the observed and predicted rainfall," says Strem, "the model produces a hydrograph with six-hour time steps on a given river out to four or five days." The Sacramento model is typically run on relatively large basins to chart longer-term river flooding, but it can also generate smaller-scale flash-flood guidance for NWS forecasters. With the model's help, Strem says, "the NWS will know how much rain it's going to take to start causing problems."

Two situations go beyond the model capabilities. One is how to deal with the smallest-scale flash floods caused by urbanization or other land-use changes. The other is when levees and dams give way. This happened with disconcerting frequency [in the] winter [of 1997] in central California and again [in the] spring with the Red River of the North flood that devastated Grand Forks, North Dakota. In such cases, a slow-cresting river flood can suddenly become a flash flood, and present computer models cannot predict where the newly rechanneled water will go.

Flood Disasters

The Infamous Johnstown Flood

By David M. Ludlum

The Johnstown Flood of 1889 is one of the top three natural disasters in United States history, according to David M. Ludlum in the following selection. A flash flood created by heavy rains and an ensuing fire killed over twenty-one hundred people in Johnstown, a manufacturing city of about thirty thousand residents, situated in the Allegheny Mountains of Pennsylvania. Ludlum, an authority on American weather history, reports that heavy rains inundated the nearby Conemaugh River, raising it over twenty feet and causing the collapse of an earthen dam fifteen miles upstream. Together with the dam waters, the swollen river scoured the valley, destroying everything in its path. The waters eventually deposited a thirty acre pile of debris against a stone bridge in downtown Johnstown; the pile eventually caught fire, killing those who had sought refuge on the bridge. Despite flood control efforts following the disaster, the river flooded again in 1977, killing at least seventy-six more people.

The three worst natural disasters in American history are the Johnstown Flood, the Galveston Hurricane, and the San Francisco Earthquake and Fire. Of the three, the Johnstown Flood is arguably the most infamous.

No resident of the Conemaugh Valley suspected the deadly seriousness of the sequence of events set in motion when the first drops of light rain began falling over the Allegheny Mountains of west-central Pennsylvania on the quiet Memorial Day afternoon of Thursday, May 30, 1889. They were the harbinger of a band of increasingly heavy rain generated by a slow-moving storm system approaching from the west by way of the Ohio Valley.

Though not of great barometric depth, the narrow weather trough extended southward like a long finger from Canada to the

Gulf of Mexico. It separated cold polar air rushing southward over the Great Lakes from warm tropical air streaming northward over the Atlantic coastal plain. Thus, nature set the stage for a clash of elements over Pennsylvania—a collision that would produce a rainstorm of great intensity. And man's defective works would compound the consequences of that elemental encounter to turn an already major flash flood into a catastrophe of unprecedented proportions.

How Much Rain Fell

Johnstown, then a manufacturing city of some 30,000 souls, is situated in a narrow river valley on the main line of the Pennsylvania Railroad, about one third of the way from Altoona to Pittsburgh. The exact amount of rain that fell on Johnstown that day cannot be determined, since the local observer, Mrs. H.M. Ogle, died in the flood.

Rainfall has been estimated at 6.2 inches by averaging nearby observations. Measured amounts ranged up to 9.8 inches (at Wellsboro in Tioga County) in the Susquehanna watershed. It is

This picture shows the remains of the South Fork Dam, which broke on May 31, 1889, causing over twenty-one hundred deaths.

likely that the higher mountains caught larger amounts.

On Friday morning, May 31, the steady rain sent the Cone-maugh River over its banks and into the factories, stores, and homes in the narrow valley above Johnstown. When the local rain gauge was carried away by high water at 10:44 A.M., the river was already 20 feet above low water; by noon it was "higher than ever known . . . ," according to the river reporter.

This was already a record flood that would have achieved his-toric local stature without the fateful events soon to occur some 15 miles upstream, at South Fork Creek of the Little Conemaugh River. A dam had been built there in 1852 to supply water for the Pennsylvania Canal. When the canal project was abandoned in favor of the railroad, the "Old Reservoir" remained unused and neglected until 1879, when a group of wealthy sportsmen bought the property to create a fishing camp. The level of the South Fork Dam was lowered two feet to make room for a trans-verse roadway, which, in turn, necessitated partial obstruction of the spillway by trestles needed to support the roadway. Wire-mesh fish guards were also installed. Despite these obstructions, the spillway had still satisfactorily carried off the discharge of the South Fork Creek—until that Friday.

The dammed stream formed a considerable body of water over two miles long and a little less than one mile across at its widest point. It covered about 450 acres. When full with spring run-off, it was close to 70 feet deep. The earthen dam impound-ing this body of water was about 900 feet long, with a crest some 72 feet above the stream bed. The surface of the water stood about 450 feet above the level of the stone bridge in the center of Johnstown.

The Dam Dissolves

By 11:30 A.M. that fateful Friday, with flood waters already rag-ing through the lower part of the valley, the rising water of the heavy run-off behind South Fork Dam reached the crest. For three hours, water surged over the dam and ate away its earthen structure. Finally, about 3 P.M., the pent-up pressure became too great. The whole dam suddenly dissolved into a muddy mass that swirled down the steep incline into the valley below, while the suddenly freed waters of the fishing lake exploded downstream to gorge the already swollen Conemaugh.

This awful moment was witnessed by the Reverend G.W.

Brown, pastor of the South Fork United Brethren Church:

> Having heard the rumor that the reservoir was leaking,
> I went up to see for myself. It was ten minutes of three.
> When I approached, the water was running over the
> breast of the dam to a depth of about a foot. The first
> break in the earthen surface, made a few minutes later,
> was large enough to admit the passage of a train of
> cars. When I witnessed this, I exclaimed, "God have
> mercy on the people below."
>
> The dam melted away. . . . Only a few minutes were re-
> quired to make an opening more than 300 feet wide
> and down to the bottom. I watched it until the wall
> that held back the waters was torn away, and the entire
> lake began to move, and finally, with a tremendous rush
> that made the hills quake, the vast body of water . . .
> poured . . . into the valley below. Only about 45 min-
> utes were required to precipitate those millions of tons
> of water upon the unsuspecting inhabitants of the
> Conemaugh valley. Onward dashed the flood, roaring
> like a mighty battle, treetop high, toward South Fork
> village, rolling over and over again rocks that weighed
> tons and tons, carrying them a mile or more from the
> spot where they had lain for ages.

The Death Mist

Most people never saw the wall of water coming, but they heard
it—a deep, steady rumble that grew louder and louder until it
roared like thunder. The few who did see the approaching water
and lived to tell about it were impressed by the cloud of dark
spray that hung over the front of the wave.

One survivor reported "a blur, an advance guard, . . . a mist,
like dust that precedes a cavalry charge." Another thought at first
that there must have been a terrible explosion or fire up river,
"for the water coming down looked like a cloud of the blackest
smoke I ever saw." "The awful mass of spray," long remembered
by the lucky survivors, was later referred to as "the death mist."

The rush of water from the South Fork joined the already
flooded mainstream to form a sloping wall of water as much as
20 to 30 feet high. This "water glacier" scoured the river valley
clean all the way down to Johnstown, traveling at the extraordi-

nary speed (for water) of 22 feet per second. Every tree and tele-
graph pole, every home, store, and factory, as well as locomotives,
train cars, and some 50 miles of railroad ties, rails, and roadbed in
the path of this massive torrent were all swept away, finally coming to rest in a huge, 30-acre jumble of debris jammed against the
stone arch bridge that spanned the river in downtown Johnstown.

The Debris Catches on Fire

For a time, the bridge area was an island of safety and hope for
hundreds of people and animals carried downstream on floating
debris; but the jam soon caught fire and in the holocaust that followed, many who had survived the water perished in the flames,
just as rescue was near.

All told, more than 2100 people lost their lives in this unprecedented disaster, which evoked worldwide horror and sym-
pathy.

Although many rainstorms have deluged the Allegheny
Mountains of Pennsylvania in the past 100 years, none ap-
proached the magnitude of the 1889 catastrophe—until the summer of 1977.

Rain began falling on the evening of July 19, and in the next
seven hours a rain gauge in Johnstown caught 8.5 inches, with a
total of 12 inches reported in the area—over two inches more
than fell in 1889. And despite extensive flood control measures
taken in between, the Conemaugh River and its tributaries again
surged through the city of 42,000. At least 76 people were
drowned, and property damage exceeded $100 million.

The question is: Have we yet seen the worst flash flood that
can threaten the Conemaugh Valley?

The Flooding of Galveston: The Worst Natural Disaster in U.S. History

BY ERNEST ZEBROWSKI JR.

The flooding of the island city of Galveston on September 8, 1900, is the most deadly natural disaster recorded in U.S. history. Hurricane-driven storm waves flooded the entire island with ten feet of water, drowning between six and eight thousand residents, and possibly killing four thousand more in nearby areas. Science professor Ernest Zebrowski Jr. explains in this selection, exerpted from his book Perils of a Restless Planet: Scientific Perspectives on Natural Disasters, *that Galveston, an unstable barrier island near Houston, Texas, is subject to high-energy waves which slowly but continually reshape the island. Galveston's location also makes it susceptible to tropical storms and hurricanes. Despite these conditions, a group of investors decided to develop the island. Although Galveston suffered several floodings prior to the 1900 disaster, city managers decided to make periodic repairs instead of building an expensive seawall to protect the city. However, following the 1900 flood, engineers suggested raising the entire city and building an extensive seawall. Builders undertook these plans in what was one of the most amazing engineering feats of the early twentieth century.*

Ernest Zebrowski Jr. is a professor of science and mathematics education at Southern University in Baton Rouge, Louisiana. He lectures and writes extensively about natural disasters and has written several books, including three textbooks on applied physics.

Oh the evening of September 8, 1900, hurricane-driven storm waves drowned between 6,000 and 8,000 residents of the island city of Galveston, population 37,789. In terms of lives lost, this event continues to hold the record as the worst natural disaster in U.S. history. Some 3,600 houses and hundreds of other buildings were totally destroyed, and no human structure in the city completely escaped damage. In nearby areas, the angry seas may have claimed up to an additional 4,000 lives.

Looking at a coastal map of the United States, one notices a string of long, narrow barrier islands extending down the entire eastern seaboard from New Jersey to southern Florida. Similar islands are found off the Gulf coast of south-central Florida, the stretch from the Florida panhandle to Louisiana, and along the complete length of the Gulf coast of Texas. Barrier islands are essentially very high sand bars that have been built up by wave action near coasts where the sea bottom slopes quite gradually. No barrier islands, or even beaches for that matter, are found along low-energy coastlines; the 210 kilometers (130 mi) of Florida's Gulf coast between Apalachee Bay and Crystal Bay, for instance, is lined only with heavy thickets of mangroves. Wherever one finds a barrier island, one is assured that the region is occasionally pounded by high-energy waves. One is also assured that, given the passage of enough time (say several centuries), every barrier island will be reshaped considerably as it creeps slowly toward the mainland. The lighthouse at Cape Hatteras, for instance, which in 1870 stood 460 meters from the water, by 1995 stood less than 60 meters from an often-angry surf. In 125 years, this particular barrier island beach receded the length of four football fields, while the opposite side of the island grew.

Early settlers were quick to recognize the instabilities of barrier islands, and few of them were foolhardy enough to build a permanent settlement on these shifting piles of sand. In 1838, however, a group of investors formed the Galveston City Company and began dividing up the real estate of Galveston Island, a barrier island near Houston, Texas. The venture was a huge success, and the new city thrived as a major shipping port. By 1900, a single five-block span of mansions boasted twenty-six millionaires.

Earlier Floods in Galveston

At that time (this is no longer the case), the highest ground in the city of Galveston measured just 2.7 meters (8.7 ft) above mean sea level, or less than one story. From this point, the island tapered down to Galveston Bay on the northwest and the Gulf of Mexico on the southeast. Although the living quarters of many houses began at a height of only a meter or so above sea level, this seldom created a problem, because the tides themselves usually rose and fell only 0.6 meters or less. Occasionally, however, a tropical storm would raise the seas enough to flood the city. This happened three times in 1871 (stranding a schooner and three sloops in the city streets), again in 1875 (when the sea level rose 4 meters above normal and completely flooded the island), and in 1886, when there was a considerable loss of life on the mainland but only minor damage in Galveston. After the 1886 event, a commission considered building a seawall to protect the city but rejected the idea as too costly. Repairing minor damage every decade or so was expected to be much cheaper in the long run than incurring the cost of building and perpetually maintaining a seawall.

There is very little seismic activity in the Gulf of Mexico, and no tsunami has occurred in this region in historical times. On the other hand, tropical storms and hurricanes are quite common in the Gulf. The low barometric pressure associated with such storms often raises the sea level to a considerable height over a very wide area, and wind-driven waves riding on top of such a "storm surge" or "storm swell" can be every bit as devastating as a great tsunami. The effect is particularly disastrous when the storm passes through slowly rather than quickly.

This was the case with the hurricane of September 8, 1900. We don't really know the peak wind speed, because the Weather Bureau's wind gauge blew away when the winds hit 84 miles per hour at 5:15 PM, and the storm continued well into the night. Judging from the nature of the wind damage, however, it seems unlikely that this hurricane ever produced sustained winds much in excess of 100 miles per hour. Virtually all of the devastation was caused by sea waves rather than wind.

The Hurricane Arrives

The unnamed hurricane's arrival was no surprise, for the local meteorologist had been receiving regular telegrams over the previous few days giving updates on the storm's progress through the Atlantic, from its glancing blow on southern Florida to its entrance into the Gulf of Mexico. The previous afternoon, he'd already noted minor flooding on the lowest parts of the island, despite the brisk offshore wind from the north (a condition that normally reduces the tides rather than exaggerating them). City residents, however, were not particularly alarmed, and no one felt it necessary to evacuate the island. On the morning of September 8, with the barometer dropping and a heavy rain falling, most workers still went to their jobs, and many women and children went to the beach to watch the pounding breakers. By early afternoon, when the wind speed first broke into the hurricane category (119 km/h or 74 mi/h), all shoreline structures had already been demolished by the waves, and a huge wall of debris was being driven farther into the city by each successive impact of the relentless breakers. It was now too late to evacuate, for no boat or barge had any chance of surviving a transit to the mainland.

By 6 PM, the sea was rising three-quarters of a meter (2.6 ft) per hour, and the wind was beginning to shift to the east. At 7:30 PM, in one great surge the sea level jumped 1.20 meters (4 ft) in just 4 seconds. The eye of the hurricane apparently passed just west of the island sometime between 8 and 9 PM. By this time, the entire island was under water at least 3 meters (10 ft) deep, and many of the waves rose 6 or 7 meters higher. For sev-

Between six and eight thousand people died in the Galveston flood when the city was flooded by hurricane-driven storm waves. This picture shows one of the city streets after the flood.

eral terrible hours Galveston Island ceased to exist, and the fate of the living depended on the durability of those taller buildings whose upper stories poked above the frothing sea. The waves ripped up long sections of streetcar tracks, still lashed together with ties, and battered them into rows of houses that quickly broke into splinters. A giant wall of debris, several stories high and roughly parallel to the beach, ultimately anchored itself about six blocks inland. From here to the original shoreline, everything was scoured clean by the waves. Serendipitously, the great wall of wreckage acted as a breakwater that for several hours protected the rest of the city from total destruction. Around 1:45 AM, the sea began to subside.

The next morning, survivors found one-third of the island scraped clean and the remainder battered almost beyond recognition. Everything was covered by a thick, foul-smelling slime. One observer counted forty-eight bodies dangling in the trusswork of a partially demolished railroad trestle. Initial attempts were made to bury the thousands of corpses at sea, but when the bodies began to wash back up on the beach it became necessary to stack them on the mountains of debris and burn them. From one end of the island to the other, these funeral pyres burned continually for several days and nights.

Preventing a Future Catastrophe

The horrors of the disaster drove many survivors from the island, never to return. Property values, for those structures that remained standing, plummeted to ten cents on a dollar. The next year, however, when it was apparent that Galveston was indeed going to rebuild, a board of engineers was commissioned to do an in-depth study of the disaster and to make a recommendation on how such a catastrophe might be prevented in the future. In January of 1902, these engineers delivered their report, which included the audacious recommendation that the entire city should be raised in elevation as much as 3.4 meters (11 ft) and walled off from the sea.

What followed was one of the most amazing engineering feats of the early twentieth century. To carry in heavy machinery, materials, and fill dirt, temporary railroads and canals were constructed throughout the length and width of the city. Large masonry structures like St. Patrick's Church, which weighed some 3,000 tons, were lifted on hundreds of hydraulic jacks as new foundations were built beneath them. Almost three thousand buildings were raised in this manner. At the same time, it was necessary to relocate water and sewer lines, electric lines, streets, sidewalks, trees, and gardens, all without making it impossible for residents to go about their daily business.

A concrete seawall was built along the Gulf, 4.9 meters (16 ft) wide at its base, 1.5 meters (5 ft) wide at the top, and extending to a height of 5.2 meters (17 ft) above mean low tide, its seaward face concave, so that it would deflect waves upward rather than allowing them to bear against it with their full force. On the seaward side of the wall, an 8.2-meter (27-ft) apron of granite riprap was laid over the beach to further sap the energy from any large waves. The city side was backfilled with sand to give it a gentle slope down to the level of the top of the wall. The initial seawall was 5 kilometers (about 3 mi) long; it was later extended, so that it now runs a total length of 16.15 kilometers (10.04 mi). Raising the city and completing the initial section of seawall took almost seven years.

This engineering project has demonstrated its effectiveness in several hurricanes, the first of these in 1909, before the wall was even completed. Today, beyond the western end of the wall, even a casual observer will notice that the unprotected beach has eroded inland about 50 meters (160 ft). In front of the wall, however, there is no longer any beach at all: only riprap.

Clearly, it is not economically feasible to protect every inhabited barrier island with an engineering project of the scope of Galveston's, nor would the residents of recreational beachside communities be pleased with the result: destroying the beach to save the homes. To build on a barrier island is to assume a risk. The waves will come, the beaches will creep, and flooding from the sea will someday innundate all coastal structures we build in such places. The gamble homebuilders take is that damaging sea waves are not likely to strike soon. But then again, they just might. Our modern science remains woefully inadequate when we use it to try to predict what Mother Nature might have up her sleeve during our lifetimes.

The Great Flood of 1993

BY ALAN MAIRSON

Floods are a fact of life in the Midwest, but in the spring and summer of 1993 the unusually long rains in the upper Mississippi River basin created what came to be called the "Great Flood of '93." In this selection, National Geographic *writer and editor Alan Mairson reports that it was the worst flooding to occur in the area in over thirty years. Record water levels put parts of nine states underwater, prompting President Bill Clinton to declare the floods a major disaster. An estimated fifty people were killed, seventy-two thousand homes were affected, and crop and property damages added up to more than $10 billion. Because rivers became so treacherous, the Coast Guard prohibited boat traffic on five hundred miles of the Mississippi River.*

Mairson details the events that unfolded on the farms of East Hardin, Illinois, and in the town of Hardin, where the Illinois River overflowed its banks. He provides a glimpse into the lives of local residents as they battled the rising waters. After the floodwaters destroyed levees, homes, and businesses, they receded in mid-August, leaving residents with the tough question of whether to clean up and rebuild in the ruined areas or to start over on higher ground.

On a typical July day at Jeff Lorton's farm in East Hardin, Illinois, the chores get divided up something like this: Jeff grinds corn for his 3,000 hogs while his wife, Sandy, gives the baby pigs their shots. The Lortons' teenage boys—J.D., Nate, and Laef—feed and water the livestock while 15-year-old Danielle makes the midday meal: pork steaks, mashed potatoes with gravy, white cake, and ice cream.

But the summer [of 1993] was far from typical. Record rains drenched the upper Mississippi River basin, causing widespread

Alan Mairson, "Great Flood of '93," *National Geographic*, vol. 185, January 1994, pp. 51–81. Copyright © 1994 by National Geographic Society. Reproduced by permission.

destruction. By late June the Mississippi had jumped its banks in Minnesota, where the National Guard helped battle the worst flooding in 30 years. The disaster moved downstream as the summer wore on. By early July parts of nine states, including Iowa, Missouri, and Illinois, were underwater. By mid-July, when I arrived in East Hardin, the Illinois River was rising to a record level, threatening to bring the Great Flood of '93 to the Lortons' farm.

So Jeff, Sandy, and the kids prepared for the worst. They had already moved their feed, farm tools, and all the furnishings from the first floor of their house to a relative's place across the river, and the hogs had been safely fenced in a temporary pen on higher ground nearby. A few days later the Lortons and I climbed into three pickup trucks and dashed back to their farm to grab a few more belongings.

"I rode over to look at the levee this morning, and the water's coming up too fast," Jeff said, referring to the Nutwood Levee—a 12-mile-long earthen barrier, which was the only thing standing between Jeff's 237-acre farm and the flood.

"The levee's not gonna break, is it?" Danielle asked as we loaded up the trucks.

"Nah," said Jeff confidently as he hustled upstairs. "And if it does, they'll put on the sirens and we'll get out. We'll have lots of time to get out."

We pulled armloads of clothes out of the closets and dumped them in the trucks. We hauled out mattresses and box springs and bedroom bureaus. We tossed blankets and hockey sticks and assorted odds and ends on shelves, on the pool table, on any flat surface a few feet above the second floor.

Just before we left, Jeff looked around the first floor for anything else of value. He saw the kitchen telephone and angrily ripped it off the wall. Then we piled into the trucks and crunched down the gravel drive for the last time. I looked back at the house and saw a wooden sign. "Lorton Family Farm," it said. "Welcome to Paradise."

Floods Are Frequent in the Midwest

Floods are a fact of life in the Midwest. They usually arrive in the spring, when rain and snowmelt fill the streams and rivers that drain the upper Mississippi River basin.

But the summer [of 1993], when the soil was still saturated from the spring rains, something peculiar happened: The jet stream swung south, and cool, dry air dropped down from Canada, colliding with warm, moist air pumped north into the central plains from the Gulf of Mexico. The resulting thunderstorms would normally have swept off to the east but were blocked by a high-pressure system called a Bermuda high, which had stalled over the East Coast. The storms stayed put, and the rains kept coming . . . and coming.

Places like Cedar Rapids, Iowa, got doused with nearly three feet of rain from April through July—a year's worth in four months. Concordia, Kansas, had more than twice its normal rainfall in the same period. The summer of '93 was the wettest on record for Minnesota, Illinois, Iowa, and the Dakotas and was much wetter than normal for the entire region.

With the rivers running high, the U. S. Army Corps of Engineers could no longer operate its locks and dams on the Mississippi, so it began closing them in late June, stopping all barge traffic north of Cairo, Illinois. Normally placid rivers became so treacherous that the Coast Guard prohibited virtually all boat traffic on 500 miles of the Mississippi between St. Paul, Minnesota, and St. Louis, Missouri. In Des Moines, Iowa, the Raccoon River overran its banks and knocked out the city's supply of drinking water for more than two weeks. Circumstances like these prompted President Bill Clinton to declare a major disaster in large parts of Illinois, Kansas, Minnesota, Missouri, the Dakotas, Nebraska, Wisconsin, and in all of Iowa.

A Full-Scale Military Campaign

Mid-disaster, I stopped by the Army Corps of Engineers' Emergency Operations Center in St. Louis. Telephones jangled continually, a television was tuned to the local news, and the walls were covered with oversize maps showing river levels and major levees. It was as if a full-scale military campaign was being waged up and down the river.

"We're trying to advise people as this thing unfolds," said Emmett Hahn, chief of the operations center, pointing to his assistants working the telephones. "One of them is responsible for allocating sandbags. One is in charge of water pumps. One coordinates our helicopters for reconnaissance flights. And one does situation reports."

Hahn told me he'd already worked 38 consecutive days, and he looked it. His face was gray and gaunt, and his eyes were bleary from lack of sleep. The freak weather, the size of the flood zone, the fact that the Mississippi and Missouri Rivers were going to meet and crest at the same time, creating even higher water—it was enough to keep anyone awake.

"This is like watching a disaster movie like *The Towering Inferno*," said Hahn. "You leave the movie thinking, 'That was exciting, but it would never happen in real life because you couldn't have all those events at one time.' But that's what's happened."

A disaster movie . . . maybe that was the inspiration for the message I had seen scrawled on a blackboard at a National Guard Armory: "The Mississippi," it said. "Coming soon to a town near you."

Fighting the Flood

More than a week before Jeff Lorton and his family had cleared out their bedroom closets, the fear of flood had gripped their community. The Illinois River, which separates the town of Hardin from the farms of East Hardin, normally flows 20 miles south before emptying into the Mississippi River. With all the rain, the Mississippi was already far too full, so it backed up along the Illinois River, which swelled like a blocked blood vessel.

People here fought the flood on two fronts. On the east side of the river they filled sandbags and stacked them, mile after mile, on top of the Nutwood Levee to build it higher. Usually the levee stands 21 feet above the river, but by mid-July water was licking the top. National Guardsmen pitched in to help, as did local housewives, farmers, children, retired folks, businessmen, and inmates from a nearby correctional center. Trucks and all-terrain vehicles would have been a big help hauling sandbags to critical spots on the levee, but they stood idly by: The earth was so saturated that engineers feared the vehicles' weight would cause the levee to collapse. It was slow, strenuous going.

"I did more physical work yesterday than I've done since I did a 26-mile road march in the Marine Corps," said Capt. Pat Smallwood of the Illinois National Guard. He looked over his company, sweating in the sun. "These people are really kicking butt. No whining, no complaining."

On the other side of the river, where there was no levee, people battled block by block, building by building, trying to keep the river at bay. The Hardin Drive-In, a local restaurant, looked like a bunker. It was surrounded by water and by sandbags that almost reached the roof. I could see someone scurrying around inside, monitoring the water pumps that pushed the river back out faster than it seeped in.

"We've already lost the nursing home, the medical center, and the grain elevator," Mayor Bill Horman told me. "Now we're just trying to keep the secondary roads open so people can get out of the county."

To that end, orange trucks from the Illinois Department of Transportation barreled into town, dumping tons of crushed stone on low-lying roads to elevate them and keep them dry. Park Street, one of the main routes out of town, was more than six feet high.

Water Contamination

Concerned that the rising river might contaminate the town's well, the Calhoun County Health Department instructed people to boil their tap water before using it. Tetanus shots were recommended too; the river had run into sewers, which backed up through toilets and bathtubs, down the halls, and out into the streets.

"We're telling parents to keep their kids out of the water, but it's so inviting when it's so hot," said nurse Judy Zahrli, who was giving free tetanus shots in the hallway outside the school cafeteria.

Inside, local women served home-cooked meals, brought from all over Calhoun County, to 1,500 people a day. Gena Sievers brought her barbecued pork; Evie Nolte made scalloped potatoes; the pickled beets and the brownies were courtesy of Vera Tepen; and Mary Schneider brought fresh tomatoes from her garden.

The daylight had disappeared, but the heat lingered when I joined 20 people sandbagging at the corner of Park and Franklin Streets. Porch lights from houses glittered on the water and broke the darkness. We worked in pairs—one person held an empty bag, the other shoveled in sand. We heaved the bags onto a forklift, which trundled down the street with a full load, shored up a bunker, and came back for more. For a while I worked with Al Parker, from the house on the corner. Then with Kristine Blahut, who saw the flooding on television and drove seven hours from Indianapolis with a friend to help.

The National Guard coordinated the delivery of truckloads of sand. A neighbor brought us sandwiches and cold drinks. And from a radio in the pickup truck parked on the sidewalk came song after song, two of which I still remember: "Fool on the Hill," by the Beatles, and the Animals' "We Gotta Get Out of This Place."

We shoveled and sweated. Midnight came and went. Thunder and lightning rolled in from the west. Then more rain. The river crept up the street. It didn't look particularly powerful or menacing, more like the edge of a big puddle—shallow, calm, seemingly harmless.

The Flood Spreads

The next day—July 18—water overtopped the Nutwood Levee on the other side of the river. On a hillside overlooking the levee district, local residents gathered to watch the flood. They were subdued, though not visibly depressed. Stretched out on the grass with cold beer and sandwiches, they chatted and commiserated as the disaster unfolded before them.

In the distance the Illinois River spilled over the levee's low spots, then sliced through the sodden earth like hot tea through a mound of sugar. The gash widened and brown water spread over the fields of corn and soybeans, around houses and barns. It inched north toward East Hardin, flushing out a deer, which raced away from the flood's leading edge.

"Crop insurance?" said one farmer when I asked about his coverage. "If you've farmed 70 years and never had this problem, you don't figure you need it. The levee is the crop insurance." The farmers beside him stared out at the water, poker-faced.

That evening the river's long, dark fingers slid over the road leading to the Joe Page Bridge. Slowly, deliberately, the river closed its hand around lawn ornaments, abandoned cars, mobile homes, and a few businesses.

Back in Hardin the next morning, four people on Cemetery Hill were gazing over more than 11,000 acres of flooded farmland they call the Bottoms.

"Whose house is that?" said one, pointing to a distant rooftop poking out of the water.

"I'm glad it ain't mine," said another.

"I heard Jim and Peg's caved in."

"I heard Papa's Pizza fell off its foundation."

Down at the canteen, Jeff and Sandy were anxiously trying to find out what had happened to their farm. Ed Hazelwonder, a neighbor, had just returned from inspecting the flooded area, and Jeff pulled him aside.

"How high on my second story?" asked Jeff.

"It's almost up to the window," Ed answered.

Jeff looked at Sandy. "It's over that stuff we left in the bedrooms," he said grimly.

Her lip trembled. "Nathan's stuff is lost?"

Jeff didn't answer but dashed off in search of a boat while I waited behind with Sandy.

"I dreamt about the flood," she said. "I woke up hoping it was just a dream. I literally pinched myself. I didn't want it to be true."

That afternoon we went back to the Lortons' farm, docking our boat outside the second-floor window. Jeff punched out the screen, climbed inside, and waded through thigh-deep water, high-stepping over the carpets, which had floated free of the floor.

"I can still shoot a game of pool," Jeff yelled when he saw that the top of the billiard table was still above water. Out in the boat,

Spring floods are common in towns along the Mississippi River. This picture was taken during flooding in Missouri in 1973.

I listened to him sloshing around and tried hard to think of something comforting to say to Sandy, who sat tearfully behind me. But what do you tell someone who has 14 feet of water in her house?

Jeff returned with a cardboard box filled with family photo albums, yearbooks, and football trophies his boys had won. Then we puttered back toward town, across the bottomlands, brushing the tops of ruined cornstalks, past concrete septic tanks floating free on a lakelike expanse, past empty sandbags that the flood fighters never had a chance to fill.

The Nature of the Beast

Later in the summer I would return to Hardin, but for the moment I followed the flood south toward St. Louis. The three rivers that converge near here—the Illinois, Missouri, and Mississippi—seemed to function as one live, pulsating organism with a will of its own, rising here, falling there, breaking this levee and sparing that one. Water might push and probe and knock over a community's defenses, then suddenly reverse direction and flow upstream through yet another levee break. Although you couldn't predict exactly when an area might flood and precisely who would get hit, certain patterns were immediately apparent.

"The majority of the people affected by this flood are poor," a disaster-relief expert told me. "They live where land and housing are cheap—in low-lying areas. That's the nature of the beast."

The suffering was immense—an estimated 50 people dead, 72,000 homes and 36,000 square miles affected, and more than ten billion dollars' worth of damage to crops and property. Yet the flood didn't cause violent, wholesale destruction or bring the Midwest to a sudden stop.

"After Hurricane Andrew a wide area was absolutely devastated," said Roger Schrage, relief operations manager for World Vision, which provides humanitarian assistance around the globe. "With a flood you may have a totally functioning society a hundred yards away, with supermarkets, medical services, and communications."

I knew what he meant. When I arrived in south St. Louis late in July, there were roadblocks and National Guardsmen along the River Des Peres Drainage Channel, which had flooded and forced the evacuation of thousands of homes.

A few blocks away a convenience store was open. So was a pawnshop and a gas station. And just 15 minutes from where people were building a levee of crushed stone along Germania Street, I saw tourists in downtown St. Louis at the Gateway Arch, gawking at the river, and baseball fans strolling into Busch Stadium to root for the Cardinals against the Mets. Life went on.

Yet no matter where people lived, whether their basements were wet or dry, they all seemed to have water on the brain. Where was it raining? When would the river crest? Any levee breaks recently? Every day the *St. Louis Post-Dispatch* featured a full-page spread on the flood, which included area-by-area summaries, phone numbers to get or give help, and a map with bar graphs listing the water levels along the rivers. When television weathermen pointed to a heavy thunderstorm in North Dakota or Iowa, everyone downstream knew that another surge of water would pulse through the system and eventually get to them. In the interim, people had time to prepare—and time to worry.

"Hurricanes are devastating, but at least they're over with quickly," said Ronald Van, a community-relations official with the Federal Emergency Management Agency (FEMA). "This is cruel. It just sits around. . . ."

The Floodwater Lingers

When I returned to Hardin in late July, the whole town seemed on edge. The farmland east of the Nutwood Levee was still underwater, and a storm had finally knocked out the remaining sandbag fortifications downtown. Although the rains had finally stopped, the floodwater lingered, hanging around like a smelly, boorish, uninvited houseguest. It buckled floors, soaked through walls, and frayed people's nerves.

"We can't get to the next phase of recovery until the water's out of the houses," said Carol Theler, a volunteer who ran the Red Cross Relief Center and Shelter nearby. "We go to Plan C, then Plan D, then Plan E. We're running out of letters of the alphabet. Everybody's frustrated."

With high water still blocking the Joe Page Bridge, Hardin's residents were forced to commute long distances on and off their peninsula. What used to be an 18-mile trip to the nearest good-size town, Jerseyville, now required a hundred-mile detour, much of it over unpaved country roads.

To shorten the supply line, the National Guard flew a chopper to Hardin several times a day, airlifting food, drinking water, disposable diapers, insect repellent, and, one day, a couple of detectives from Kansas. They had an arrest warrant for a murder suspect, but they couldn't find him.

"Things are getting a bit tense," said resident Jill Smith, who had stopped by the grade school with her video camera to get some shots of all the free food available in the gymnasium. "I think they should start putting tranquilizers in the water."

The public pool was shut. The county fair had been canceled. And many local businesses were struggling—or had closed.

"Business stinks," said Corbett Miller, co-owner of the local Ford dealership. "We laid off half our crew and haven't sold a new car in the county since the beginning of July."

Down at the county offices, treasurer Curt Robeen looked glum, surrounded by stacks of property-tax notices. They had been stamped and ready to mail for at least two weeks.

"I'm afraid to send them out," he said.

Cleaning Up

The water finally began to retreat from Hardin in mid-August. On the east side the river was draining out the same way it had come in—through a hole in the Nutwood Levee. In downtown Hardin the river slowly slipped back into its bed.

Yet it left its muddy mark behind. A skirt of dried scum stained the sides of every building touched by the river. Trees, stripped of their leaves, were naked from their waists down. Houses sagged and stank, as if they'd aged a hundred years in just a few weeks.

On Kennedy Street I found Dennis and Beth Kronable cleaning up her mother's house. Although four feet of water had filled the first floor, the walls were ruined up to the ceiling; the insulation had wicked the water high above the flood line, dappling the white drywall with green and black splotches of mold.

Dennis and Beth peeled away the drenched drywall, soft as an overripe banana skin, and pulled out the insulation. They removed mud-caked kitchen appliances and bathroom fixtures, hosed down the floors, and shoveled out debris.

Luckily, they had some help from the Southern Baptist disaster-relief program, which had sent volunteers from North Carolina to Hardin a few weeks earlier. They had arrived with a tractor trailer equipped to prepare hundreds of meals every day, giving the local women at the canteen a much needed rest.

"Those guys," said Beth, "'angels from heaven,' we call them.

I don't know what we'd do without 'em."

They would probably rely on the Red Cross, the Salvation Army, or the gaggle of government agencies—FEMA, the Small Business Administration, the Soil Conservation Service, among others—that had come to Hardin offering disaster relief. Soon Washington would authorize 5.7 billion dollars to help flood victims in the Midwest.

Decisions About Where to Live

Some people in East Hardin would go right back to their old homes and rebuild, using whatever assistance they could get.

For instance, I met Gene Snyders at a Red Cross disaster-assistance center, where he was applying for vouchers to buy food and clothing. His trailer had been wiped out, but he planned on moving back to the Bottoms as soon as he could find another trailer.

"I've got 46 years in that place," he said, looking me square in the eye. "That's home to me. I'm not crazy about moving somewhere else."

Ruth Johnson, also from East Hardin, wasn't certain where she would live but knew one thing for sure—she would never return to her old house, where she had lived for almost 20 years with her husband and four children.

"Even if we have to start broke all over again, we will not go back. That house is dead," she said. "I will leave it in its watery coffin, and I won't go back."

By the time I caught up with Jeff Lorton again, he looked happier than I had seen him all summer. He had just purchased 15 acres of land on the top of Rocky Hill, where, high above the floodplain, he planned to build a new home.

We hopped in my car and drove away from the river, up a steep road for a mile or so. Near the top of the hill we stopped and got out. A bulldozer was plowing a path for Jeff's new driveway.

"That's my old place way over there," he said, pointing through the haze to the Bottoms, still underwater. "We'll keep the hogs down there, and we'll work down there, but we'll live up here."

He turned and faced the bulldozer. "My driveway will come up this way," he said, tracing the path with a sweep of his arm. "And I'll put the new house right here." We were standing on his future front lawn. "The house'll be exactly like our old one, except I'll move the living room so we'll have a better view."

That's Jeff's plan, anyway. It all depends on when—and if—his flood insurance policy pays off.

If he's lucky, then sometime soon a typical summer day with the Lortons should look something like this: After Jeff, Sandy, and the boys finish their morning chores, they'll drive up Rocky Hill for their big midday meal. Off to the east, they'll see hills, green with foliage, and farmers riding tractors in the fields below. Cars will come and go across the Joe Page Bridge, and barges will work the Illinois River. And the river itself will be back within its banks, muddy and meek and right on course, slipping silently beside the floodplain it had briefly reclaimed.

It promises to be a beautiful view—as long as the weather holds.

Bangladesh's Worst Flood of the Twentieth Century

By Abdul Hannan

Bangladesh, a small country to the east of India, experienced its worst floods of the century in July, August, and September of 1998, according to Abdul Hannan, a writer for the New Internationalist, *reporting immediately after the flood. Although villagers usually welcome regular floods because the waters deposit crop-enhancing silt, the 1998 flood left 20 million homes damaged or destroyed and 60 percent of the country submerged. Villagers were left with no jobs, income, or food, and many survived by living on rafts for two months. According to Hannan, the Brahmaputra River overflowed due to unusually large amounts of rainfall. He claims that the flood problems that followed were compounded because of the country's location astride two grinding tectonic plates, which triggered troublesome seismic events that prevented floodwaters from flowing into the sea. In addition, Hannan explains that Bangladesh's corrupt political environment hindered efforts to deal effectively with the crisis.*

Villagers on Char Ishapasha heaved a sigh of relief when the flood waters started to recede [in] September [1998]. For two months, the inhabitants of this island had survived by living on rafts, while the deluge of the Brahmaputra River consumed everything in sight. Abdul Karim was one of the few who stayed to witness the spectacle. "Day after day we stayed inside using the raft for cooking and other purposes. The raft was also our only hope for survival if the house gave in to the current or the deposit level rose further."

What Abdul Karim meant by "deposit level" is evident today. An entire village on the island, home to 28 families, has been buried under some three metres of silt. This is not surprising. At its height, the Brahmaputra is known to carry tidal waves of silt, under its surface, of nine metres in height.

Floods are a staple of life. The Bangla word for it is borsha. Villagers welcome borsha, as it carries fertile silt. Nothing, however, can compare to the flood that submerged over 60 per cent of the country during the months of July, August and early September [1998]. This was borna—The Deluge. For once, even the hyperbole of journalists struggled to comprehend the enormity of the disaster. Thousands of roads, highways and lanes have been swept away in 35 of the country's 64 districts. Private property, factories and warehouses have been wrecked by standing water; tubewell water has been contaminated; bridges and culverts are unsafe to cross. According to the United Nations, 21 million people have had their homes damaged or destroyed; they are without jobs, income and food. Bangladesh, together with its development partners and the country's coterie of non-governmental organizations, has launched a colossal relief and rehabilitation operation. According to Professor Muhammad Yunus of the Grameen Bank, the only way to recover from the disaster is to "put the nation on a total war footing."

What Caused the Flood

This, the worst flood in a century, had many causes. Some 90 per cent of the water in Bangladesh originates upstream. The two main monsoon axes of the summer, one in northern India and the other in the far northeast of India, discharged unusually large volumes of rainfall for an unusually long time. Bangladesh, a country of 254 rivers, is often at the mercy of the three largest: the Ganges (or Padma, to use the local name), the Brahmaputra (Jamuna) and the Meghna. The convergence of these flows leads to a high susceptibility to flooding, especially given the country's flat topography. [In 1998], due to the lengthy duration of monsoon rains, the convergence occurred on three occasions, one after another. By the first week of September, this was aggravated by a full moon, which stalled the discharge of flood water into the Bay of Bengal.

If this was not bad enough, a series of seismic events in the Bay of Bengal during August, which resulted in a slight shift of the sea bed, are being partly blamed for preventing flood water from flowing into the deep sea. This untimely news was a reminder that Bangladesh is a new land, in geological terms. What comprises Bangladesh today has accreted rapidly over the past 6,000 years, building up layer upon layer of silt flowing down from the Himalayas. Bangladesh also sits on the cusp of two massive tectonic plates, the Indian and the Eurasian. As these grind into one another, they occasionally let off steam through tremors such as those that occurred in the Bay [in the] summer [of 1998].

Efforts to Cope Are Hindered

A fractious and corrupt political culture, combined with an unresponsive and unwieldy administration, have hindered past efforts to deal with such calamities. The last great inundation, in 1988, was followed by ill-conceived attempts to instate a Flood Action Plan. The Plan was scuppered by a powerful nongovernment organization (NGO) and environmental lobby because of its sheer lack of consultation with local people. The Flood Action Plan would have required forced resettlement of hundreds of thousands of people. Its nonparticipatory nature was ironically summed up when the Government of Bangladesh sat with its donors at a special session on "participation" in the ill-conceived Flood Action Plan in April 1994. The meeting took place behind closed doors in a five-star hotel in Dhaka. Construction work on embankments began even before environmental assessments were complete. Local people were observed breaking down the embankments of these and earlier constructions to allow flood water into their fields.

None of this will do much to help Abdul Karim and the millions of people in his predicament. But he should be warned. In the 1950s, 1970s and 1980s, disastrous floods occurred back to back. This may be a statistical illusion; then again it might not. The story goes that the animals went in two by two. In Bangladesh, it's the floods that come in pairs. Bad as things [were in 1998], there could be worse to come.

China's Epic Floods of 1998

BY DOUG REKENTHALER

The following selection was written in August 1998 in the midst of some of the worst flooding China had experienced in decades. The floods were occurring all along rivers in northeast, central, and northwest China, especially along the Yangtze, one of China's largest rivers. The government estimated the death toll at 2 thousand people and reported that 260 million had been affected by the floods. Hundreds of thousands of people took up residence on levees and were told by authorities that they might not be able to return to their homes for a month or more. In addition, health officials were extremely concerned about the possibility of outbreaks of diseases such as dysentery. This possibility increased as flood-waters lingered and the rains were expected to continue indefinitely. Some blamed the disastrous flooding on the government for allowing extensive development in the floodplains and for clear-cutting forests, a practice that filled the rivers with silt. Doug Rekenthaler is managing editor for the U.S. Disaster Relief Organization.

The epic floods spreading across China grew a little worse on Friday [August 14, 1998] after a major levee guarding the country's largest oil field collapsed, spilling billions of gallons of water into the critical northeastern area.

The breach, which by midday had eaten its way through a quarter-mile of the levee, sent thousands of people fleeing for higher ground. The government promptly mobilized more than 200,000 people to close the breach and redouble their efforts elsewhere in Daqing, where the oil field is located.

Waters on the Nen and Songhua rivers reached record heights this week [the second week in August 1998], and more than a million soldiers and civilians have been engaged in a round-the-clock battle to keep the floods at bay. Authorities said 1,000 of the field's 20,000 oil wells were closed as a result of the breach and incessant rains, and a massive campaign is under way to create an inland barrier to protect the other wells. The Daqing field produces about half of all of China's oil.

The closure of so many wells will only serve to exacerbate the growing economic toll the floods are having on China. Official estimates suggest the floods already have cost $24 billion and will reduce by at least one-half point China's gross domestic product this year.

Business and Government Are Blamed

On Thursday, *China Daily* ran a report blaming business and government leaders for advocating policies that worsened the floods, including massive development along the Yangtze and clear-cutting of forests that filled rivers with silt. "The decision-makers and local residents in the higher reaches of big rivers, the Yangtze in particular, have been chewing up lumber for money or simply for firewood and putting enormous pressure on the forest reserves," it said.

At least 20,000 residents of Heilongjiang were rescued on Friday after becoming stranded by rising water, which also has affected neighboring Russia. More than 400,000 people have been left homeless from flooding in the northeast that local authorities describe as the worst in history.

Flooding also is beginning to take its toll in the northwest, where high waters and landslides in Xinjiang on Thursday killed four people and left 100,000 homeless. Landslides in the region have severed major communications and transportation corridors, including a major rail line between Xinjiang's capital, Urumqi, and the city of Lanzhou.

Officials also are keeping a sharp eye on the Yellow River in the north, which is expected to suffer heavy flooding over the next week or more. A seemingly endless series of low pressure systems have rolled across northern stretches of China for the past two weeks, dumping record rains on many regions and feeding already dangerously high rivers and tributaries.

The Yangtze Caused Massive Flooding

Most of the country's focus and flood-fighting resources remain on the Yangtze, which has caused massive flooding throughout central China for nearly two months. A fifth major flood crest recently thundered down the central stretches of the river, although levees safeguarding major industrial cities such as Wuhan held firm. Authorities called off plans to purposely flood an area upriver that is home to 330,000 people, after the crest failed to reach the "do or die" limit by only eight inches.

But torrential rains in Sichuan have created a sixth flood crest that is beginning to make its way down the river. More than a million exhausted soldiers and civilians continue to monitor the hundreds of levees lining the river, quickly working to plug the numerous breaches that now are a daily occurrence. Concerns also are mounting that as water levels lower in some areas, the dikes could weaken, setting the stage for disaster in the event of new floods.

Hundreds of thousands of people have taken up residence on many levees, often the only high ground available. If one of the populated levees was to break, the death toll could be staggering. For now, the government only will admit that 2,000 people have been killed by the flooding, but that figure has not changed in many weeks and most feel it is severely understated. About one-in-five Chinese citizens (260 million people) have been affected by the floods, the worst to strike the country since 1954 when Yangtze flooding took the lives of 30,000.

Health Concerns

Health officials are extremely concerned about the spread of disease, which becomes more and more likely with each day that the flood waters remain. Millions of Chinese spend their days wading through waist-deep water—water that is filled with sewage and the rotting corpses of animals.

Most of the outbreaks thus far, at least by official counts, have been limited to skin conditions, eye infections, and diarrhea. However, more serious problems such as dysentery and "snail fever" could become a major problem. Major health threats are expected to arise as flood waters dissipate and cleanup begins.

Only a small percentage of victims have received water purification tablets, making clean water and food a precious commodity throughout much of the flood regions. High heat and humidity also are contributing to the fear of epidemic. Affected villagers complain that thieves are stealing relief supplies and government officials pilfering relief funds.

The International Federation of Red Cross and Red Crescent Societies only have managed to bring in about 40 percent of the $4.2 million it had hoped to raise for the relief effort. Sherilyn Amy, a spokeswoman for the organization, said: "It is becoming increasingly clear that in this disaster there is no end in sight. If we can't get funding, we can't help these people. We desperately need public support right now."

Chinese authorities have warned flood victims that they may not be able to return to their homes for a month or more. Heavy rains are expected to continue to plague the country for at least the next few weeks, and it will be some time before the water levels return to normal levels.

Averting Disaster

Skirting Disaster: Testing Flood Prevention Methods in Northern California

BY EDWIN KIESTER JR.

In the following selection journalist Edwin Kiester Jr. gives an inside look into how meteorologists, hydrologists, water-management operators, and flood fighters were put to the test at the end of 1996 when three severe rainstorms hit northern California within a week. Although there were eight deaths and the state incurred $2 billion in damages, Kiester reports that it could have been much worse. Forecasters at the Flood Operations Center in Sacramento worked around-the-clock making vital predictions about when, where, and how much rain would fall. Based on these predictions, the forecasters advised local dam operators on whether to release or hold back the voluminous amounts of water building up in reservoirs, and they issued evacuation warnings to many thousands of people in low-lying areas. Forecasters, engineers, and hydrologists used rain gauges, Doppler radar, satellite images, and National Weather Service data to make exceptionally accurate observations and predictions.

As he switched off the tree lights on Christmas night, Bill Mork headed for bed with a sense of foreboding. After five straight days of closely monitoring a snowstorm that

Edwin Kiester Jr., "Water Water Everywhere," *Smithsonian*, vol. 28, August 1997, pp. 34–44. Copyright © 1997 by Edwin Kiester Jr. Reproduced by permission.

dumped up to nine feet of snow in the Sierra Nevada, the California state meteorologist was taking a few days off. After all, his weather forecast on December 23 [1996] had shown uneventful weather right through New Year's Day. Now, two days later, television weathermen were predicting a wet weekend and storms deluging Northern California perhaps for a week.

The next morning, seated before his computer in the joint state-federal Flood Operations Center in Sacramento, Mork could see that the outlook had indeed dramatically changed. A high-pressure area centered over Alaska had caused a low-pressure area to form in the eastern North Pacific, which pulled moisture-laden subtropical air northeastward, directly toward Northern California. It was already raining, and a formidable storm, which he estimated would hit on the weekend, was approaching the coast. A second strong storm was following in its wake. Little did he know that by the 28th, a third storm would be seen lurking in the Western Pacific with ominously greater wallop.

Reviewing weather charts and computer models the next day, the 27th, Mork grew confident that the potential third storm, carrying the remnants of a Philippine typhoon, would smash into California along with the New Year. Seeking more evidence, he consulted global forecasts of the European Centre for Medium-Range Weather Forecasts in England and the British Meteorological Office. He reviewed images from U.S. and Japanese satellites. Then he looked up weather records from California's great storms of 1964 and 1986.

Mork had been forecasting California weather for 14 years, and amid the curves and circles and squiggly lines and tiny notations on the weather charts, he saw an ominously familiar pattern. The combination of a blocking high-pressure area over Alaska and a strong, warm flow from the tropics "had parallels to our historic storms of the century." California was facing a disaster.

Disastrous Floods

When "disaster" and "California" appear in the same sentence, most people think of a nervous Earth shaking buildings and bridges, or out-of-control wildfires roaring through the hills. In fact, year in and year out, nine out of ten natural disasters in the state result from floods. Historians still write with awe of 19th-century floods that turned central California into an inland sea, and of monster floods in 1955, 1964 and 1986 that cost dozens of lives and billions of dollars. Lesser floods are more frequent.

Disastrous floods, of course, are by no means peculiar to California. Floods [in 1997] in Ohio, Kentucky and North Dakota, and the 1993 inundations along the Missouri and Mississippi rivers caused tremendous destruction as well as loss of life. According to the National Weather Service (NWS), floods in the United States result in more property damage and loss of life than any other natural event. The toll in Grand Forks and along the Red River is still being tabulated. There are communities along the Mississippi and the Missouri that still have not completely recovered from 1993.

Flood Forecasting

Humans have been trying to predict riverine temper tantrums since the days of the pharaohs. Eyeball and finger-in-the-wind methods came first, eventually giving way to more sophisticated rain gauges, measuring devices in streams and volunteer observers who phoned their data to a central forecasting headquarters. Today the NWS keeps a weather eye on rivers via 13 high-tech river forecast centers, the largest of them—the California-Nevada River Forecast Center—in partnership with the state of California.

At each center, a corps of meteorologists, hydrologists, water management experts and hydraulic engineers charts every water movement to forecast when, and how emphatically, rivers might rise. Forecasters receive a constant stream of data from automated rain gauges, U.S. Geological Survey (USGS) and California Department of Water Resources (DWR) measuring stations in rivers and streams, and satellite pictures, and use Doppler radar to track storms. They plug the numbers into computer models that analyze every drop of water, degree of temperature and millibar of atmospheric pressure. They consult their own experience and horse sense. With all this, they have eliminated much of the guesswork from flood forecasting. And yet, acknowledges Maurice Roos, California's veteran chief hydrologist, flood forecasting remains an inexact science.

A nondescript office building on the edge of Sacramento houses under one roof the NWS California-Nevada River Forecast Center; the NWS Sacramento Weather Office; the hydrology branch of the DWR; the U.S. Bureau of Reclamation Central Valley Project; and the State Water Project operators, all concerned with the waters' rise and fall. On that wet Friday, De-

Flood workers rebuild a sandbag barrier in an attempt to divert flooding from the Des Moines River in 1947. While flood forecasting is now more accurate, it still remains an inexact science and towns are often unprepared for flooding.

cember 27, representatives from 20 agencies crowded into the Flood Operations Center to hear Mork's morning weather briefing. Displaying computer models, maps and rainfall figures, he told the group to brace for a one-two-three punch. The first storm would hit Sunday and produce four inches of precipitation; the second, on Monday, would add four inches more, with the third storm bringing rain through New Year's Day.

"We see a hell of a lot of rain over the next eight days," Mork said—more than 20 inches in the Feather River basin by January 2. It would follow the storm track that the media nicknamed the "Pineapple Express" because of its supposed Hawaiian origin. Temperatures would be well above freezing at elevations up to 9,000 feet, so virtually all the "precip" would fall as rain, not snow, and quickly run off—bad news when some parts of the state had already received more than two and a half times the normal precipitation for the month. Knowing that alarming the state with an inaccurate forecast could cost millions in unnecessary flood-fight mobilization, Mork nonetheless stuck with his prediction. The weather conditions were almost exactly like those that had produced the record-breaking floods of 1964 and 1986.

A call from the Flood Operations Center soon went out to Sacramento's riverside Discovery Park, where officials began to close the parking lot and turn away tourists. Then hydrologists at the center went to work. One task was to estimate the amount of water in the rivers up to 120 hours in the future—"not just how much and where," state hydrologist Gary Hester was to say, "but when." Into their computer model went the amount of rain that had fallen, the forecast of how much would fall, the route the runoff was likely to take, the measured river and reservoir inflows, and the present saturation of the ground in the watershed. Those figures were combined with measurements of current water levels at some 40 USGS stations, among others.

"The earth is like a wet kitchen sponge," says Frank Richards of the NWS Hydrologic Information Center in Silver Spring, Maryland. "The sponge can only absorb so much water and then the water rolls right off onto the floor." That certainly described Northern California on December 27. Most watersheds were sopping from storms on the previous weekend as well as earlier ones. Runoff in some areas could start virtually with the very first raindrop. It would arrive in streams that were already swollen. Additionally, a heavy snowpack, up to 11 feet, lay in the mountains. High-altitude rain and warm temperatures would mostly compact the snow rather than melt it, the model showed, but runoff from melting would be equivalent to runoff from as much as 10 percent additional precipitation.

California uses three stages of flood alerts. At the "warning" stage, patrols of levees begin and warnings go out that low-lying roads and land may be flooded. "Flood" stage for unleveed rivers indicates that there will be considerable inundation of land—the point when precautions should be taken to protect lives and property. For leveed rivers, flood stage occurs when levees reach their full capacity. A foot higher than this and the leveed water reaches the "danger" stage, at which damage to life and property is imminent. On December 27, the forecast center issued its first bulletin of this flood. The Sacramento River had risen to warning levels, or nearly so, at four places that morning.

How California Rivers Run

Some California rivers pour westward into the Pacific; others head eastward into the Nevada desert. But just over half of Northern California's precipitation funnels into the Central Valley, the huge basin extending from Shasta Dam in the north to Bakersfield in the south. The south-flowing Sacramento River, the state's largest, with its six major tributaries, and the smaller, north-flowing San Joaquin, with its own chain of mountain-fed streams, make possible the state's huge irrigated agribusiness, as well as provide water for the faucets and swimming pools of arid Southern California. Precipitation falls almost exclusively between November and April, so each raindrop and snowflake is precious and must be carefully hoarded to survive six months of dry spells.

California's water supply is thus bottled up by more than 1,400 dams and reservoirs. Five thousand miles of earthen levees, some 100 years old, imprison the often unruly rivers within their channels. Weirs and bypasses serve as flood-pressure relief valves, detouring winter waters into floodplains that become farmlands during the dry season.

Each major reservoir reserves a portion of its capacity for flood prevention. Of the 4.5 million acre-feet of storage space behind Shasta Dam, for example, 1.3 million is set aside to accommodate floodwaters. (One acre-foot is the amount of water that will cover one acre to a depth of one foot, or about 325,000 gallons.) Saving space for a wet January while husbanding enough for a dry August thus becomes an elaborate yearly minuet. "You don't want to release water too soon on the basis of a flood forecast that might not come true," says Roos. "Because once you let it go, you can never get it back." But reservoir operators don't want to be overwhelmed, either. River forecasters tell operators how much runoff to expect; operators decide how to make way for it; and forecasters predict downstream water levels—and issue flood warnings.

A Weatherman's Nightmare

On Sunday, December 29, Bill Mork woke to a weatherman's nightmare. For two days his confident predictions of forthcoming downpours had been all over the airwaves. But now, in the Sacramento Valley, only a few soft sprinkles were falling. On the phone, a fellow church choir member needled him: "What happened to that big storm you were talking about?" Mork ruefully agreed that the quarter-inch of precipitation was "underwhelming." Nearly 100 flood and emergency officials attended his morning briefing. Some of his listeners were skeptical, and a few were downright hostile.

Paul Fujitani knew better. One floor above the Flood Operations Center, Fujitani and fellow hydraulic engineers at the U.S. Bureau of Reclamation controlled five major dams and reservoirs on the Sacramento and San Joaquin rivers and their tributaries. Computerized models reaching Sacramento disclosed that, in the next few days, rain would fall by the bucketful above Shasta Dam, on the Sacramento River's northern reaches. Water would gush into the reservoir at what would become a record rate on January 1.

Fujitani's boss, Chet Bowling, knew better, too. Only a few days before, Bowling was driving north to Oregon for his wife's grandmother's 100th birthday celebration when he ran into downpours far heavier than the forecast had anticipated. Bowling immediately stopped and phoned Reclamation headquarters. Shasta Lake was already a bit swollen from the previous weekend's storms, and the bureau had begun releasing water to make room for the coming inflows. Bowling authorized increased releases ahead of the massive inflow of water. The releases had to be carefully calibrated, however, because tributaries below the dam were also pouring record amounts into the river.

Water Travels Fast in California

The 1993 floods on the Mississippi and the Missouri took days and even weeks to ceremoniously build to a crescendo, allowing downstream communities to prepare themselves for the onslaught. The Red River flooding, fed by rapid melting of unprecedented snowfall, spread gradually over the table-top-flat North Dakota landscape. But "gravity is the big player in California," Frank Richards says. Because of steep, mountainous terrain, in a mere 12 hours water released from Shasta Dam reaches Red Bluff, a major farm center about 700 feet lower and about 40 miles away. Water from the highest and rainiest parts of the Feather River watershed arrives in Sacramento in three days. Thus, on the morning of Sunday, December 29, the hydrology team at the forecast center announced that the Sacramento was already flooding at one place and had reached the warning stage at eight others.

The Sacramento had also climbed to 25 feet at the I Street Bridge in the heart of the state capital. That figure automatically summoned the Flood Operations Center to round-the-clock operation. DWR employees were mobilized to notify emergency officials and answer phone calls from worried citizens. Twenty-four-hour patrols began to watch for problems in the levees. The National Guard and prison inmates stood by for sandbagging and rescue duty.

California's dams and reservoirs are operated by a network of federal, state and local agencies, plus power companies, irrigation districts and water agencies. For example, just the Stanislaus River, a major San Joaquin tributary, is dammed in more than ten places. Each reservoir's inflow and outflow affects that of the others downstream, necessitating an intricate process of cooperation, and sometimes balky coordination, spelled out for some of the most critical Central Valley dams and reservoirs by the U.S. Army Corps of Engineers.

On Tuesday, December 31, the forecast center gave more bad news. "Heavy rain has produced a major flood on the upper Sacramento River," declared the 9 A.M. bulletin. The river was already almost a foot above the 23-foot flood stage at Red Bluff. The lower Sacramento and the Feather had each reached the warning stage in three places, and some smaller creeks were already out of their banks. Warnings had been sounded at eight places in the San Joaquin basin.

At his morning briefing, Mork could offer no respite. An overflow crowd heard a prediction of continued intense rain for the next day and a half. With the second storm continuing and the third looming just off the coast, some mountain locations had already collected a foot and a half of rain. Crews were frantically sandbagging at dozens of levees. The river models indicated that three major reservoirs might fill to the brim before the rain stopped. Chet Bowling told Shasta crews to place flashboards on top of the emergency spill gates, which would add two feet of height and hold about 60,000 more acre-feet of water.

Tools for Tracking Floods

California's rivers respond quickly to rain, so flood warnings use both observations and predictions of rainfall. In addition to rain gauges, one observational tool is Doppler radar, which tracks storms, showing heavy downpours and lighter ones in vivid colors. For prediction, California forecasters rely on NWS data as well as an ingenious computer model developed by Owen Rhea of the Sacramento NWS staff. His orographic model forecasts precipitation produced by air lifted over mountains. In it, predictions of wind, temperature and humidity up to 20,000 feet are combined with land-elevation data at three-mile intervals to pinpoint precipitation amounts and locations in the mountains. Such a tool is invaluable, as most precipitation in the Central Valley watershed falls in the mountains above the valley.

What the orographic model showed on December 31 was awesome. Ordinarily, three times as much precipitation falls in the mountains as in the Sacramento Valley. But throughout the three storms the mountains were *eight* times wetter. And with a temperature of 37 degrees Fahrenheit even at 9,000 feet, most precipitation was falling as rain and running off immediately in torrential amounts. Forecasters saw with a shudder that water would cascade down the Feather into Lake Oroville at more than 250,000 cubic feet per second (cfs)—nearly as much as the rate of the great storm of 1986. (One cubic foot is about 7.5 gallons.)

When 1997 arrived at midnight, none of the weary forecast crews felt like toasting it. Mork's third storm was delivering as promised—and then some. Mork himself drove to the center at 5 A.M. January 1. Windshield wipers could hardly keep up with the deluge; his car swerved and hydroplaned as water streamed across the highway. Mork had predicted that 6.2 inches of precipitation would fall on the Feather River basin between 4 A.M. January 1 and 4 A.M. January 2. He wondered now if he might be wrong—on the low side.

At the Flood Operations Center, Mark Heggli gazed at his computer screen with gratification and awe. Although other forecast centers depend more on volunteer weather observers, nearly all of California's data collection is automated. Heggli, a DWR meteorologist, supervised collection of data from more than 200 real-time hydrometeorological data stations in remote and rugged locations, some of which have tiny tipping buckets capturing each raindrop and sending back a signal when filled. This information was combined with the USGS data on how much water was already in the streams and rivers.

Heggli watched, fascinated by the data coming in: a bright blue line of steeply ascending dots representing rainfall. The station at La Porte, at a 5,000-foot elevation on the south fork of the Feather River, registered 6 inches of rain by 11 A.M. in a downpour that would eventually reach 11 inches for the day. Heggli switched to Bucks Lake, a notoriously wet spot where the mountain range makes a sharp turn to the west. Bucks Lake was on its way to 11 inches for the day and a whopping 42 inches for all the storms.

"Very heavy rain is producing a major flood on the upper Sacramento," an early New Year's morning forecast warned. The river was expected to rise as much as three feet above flood stage at Red Bluff and seven feet above flood stage downstream and to remain at such heights through Thursday. Farther south, a "major rise" was occurring. The leveed Feather was expected to reach flood stage at Nicolaus, 30 miles above Sacramento, and was threatening the twin towns of Yuba City and Marysville. Rivers in the San Joaquin basin had reached flood stage in three places and were at the warning stage in five others.

And still the rains came—and came.

"We were really sweating," Mork recalled later. "The inflows were exceeding anything seen this century. It scared the hell out of people. You see all this coming in and you say, 'When is it ever going to stop?'"

Engineers Sweating It

The Bureau of Reclamation engineers were particularly nervous. Despite the record amounts of water pouring into the Shasta reservoir, they had held back on releases to compensate for the uncontrolled flash flooding from creeks downstream. Earlier forecasts had predicted that water would pour into Shasta at a rate of more than 230,000 cfs, enough to fill the reservoir and have water released over the emergency spill gates. The inflow was already beyond 200,000 cfs, and the reservoir was rapidly losing precious storage space. "That was a situation you didn't want to be in," Bowling said caught between making potentially damaging releases and a possibly greater disaster—losing control of releases altogether because storage space was gone.

As did Sutter County, Yuba County—with Oroville Dam forecast to overflow and water-soaked levees along the river being pounded mercilessly—suggested people leave. Fifty thousand residents of Yuba City and Marysville were urged to head for shelters and higher ground. "For miles," as one resident later described the scene, "all it was was headlights and taillights." (In the end, the river subsided and inflows fell short of the dam top, though some levees did break.)

"We can't take another eight hours of this," Paul Fujitani remembers thinking. Then, at about 4 P.M. on New Year's afternoon, the gauges at the northern end of the Shasta watershed brought the first bit of heartening news. Rainfall, while still heavy, had definitely slackened. The orographic model and the Doppler radar showed the storm moving south and east, out of the Sacramento watershed. About 24 hours later, Shasta Dam plateaued short of overflowing its emergency spill gates.

Crews in the Flood Operations Center breathed a sigh of relief—momentarily. The Sacramento floodwaters were still rolling downstream and not expected to peak for at least 24 hours. And the storm was now bearing down with full force on the San Joaquin basin.

The San Joaquin waters some of California's richest farmland. Four major tributaries and several smaller ones flow out of the southern Sierra Nevada. In winter the San Joaquin rarely floods because most precipitation falls as snow, which melts gradually in the sunshine of spring and early summer. "When it's solid, we don't worry about it." Roos had said. But this time all the precipitation below 10,000 feet fell as rain. Turbulent, record-breaking amounts of water hammered down the steep mountainsides.

Ordinarily, the Sacramento has a mean flow of 35,000 cfs. The flow on the sinuous, slow-moving San Joaquin is about a tenth of that. Its level is often higher than the land beyond its levees. The combination of storms overwhelmed the narrow channel. The Cosumnes River, unregulated by dams, alone was dumping more than 40,000 cfs into the main channel. Below Michigan Bar, a gauging site, the Cosumnes was lapping at the doors of the firehouse in tiny Wilton.

"No one had ever seen water like that," Roos said. "The river can't tolerate that kind of inflow." "Heavy rainfall is producing a major rise on the Cosumnes River," a bulletin announced at 8:15 P.M. Wednesday, forecasting an increase to near 18 feet—6 feet above flood stage—by Thursday afternoon. The next morning's bulletin upped the forecast to 19 feet. An afternoon bulletin repeated the Cosumnes forecast and reported "major flooding" on two other rivers, the Tuolumne near Modesto and the lower San Joaquin.

An Emergency Bulletin Warning

At 1 A.M. Friday, Roos, who had gone home for a few hours' sleep, was awakened by a call from the forecast center, asking him for advice on an emergency bulletin warning of a "significant and dangerous rise on the San Joaquin and its tributaries." "Major flooding can be expected along the Tuolumne and Merced rivers," the bulletin continued. By then in Modesto, a fast-growing city of 180,000, police were going from residence to residence, urging people to flee before the Tuolumne began to swirl into riverside trailer parks and tract houses. The Merced had come up rapidly during the night in Yosemite National Park and transformed the spectacular valley into one vast lake. Water as much as five feet deep washed through first-floor rooms of the Yosemite Lodge. Bridges were ripped out and roads undermined. Picnic tables floated downstream.

Chris Kiriakou remembers that horrific afternoon well. The assistant general manager of the Turlock Irrigation District had responsibility for Don Pedro Dam on the Tuolumne. The dam holds two million acre-feet of water and in its 26-year history had never completely filled. January 3, 1997, was different. "None of us had ever seen runoffs like we experienced that day," Kiriakou says. "They were astronomical, way beyond the capacity of the channel." Kiriakou's problems were complicated by record unchecked inflows from creeks below the dam, plus heavy releases from overloaded dams upstream. "There were heavy flows from Hetch Hetchy," he said, naming the reservoir that provides much of San Francisco's water supply. Kiriakou opened the emergency spillway and release gates for the first time since the dam was built to get rid of water virtually as fast as it came in. "We were getting inflows at 122,000 cfs. We buffered as much as we could, about 60,000 cfs, but we were still putting 59,000 cfs into a 9,000-cfs channel. I felt very badly for the people downstream [in Modesto]," he said. "It was tragic for them. But it would have been many times worse if the dam had failed and brought the whole reservoir crashing down on them."

At the Bureau of Reclamation's Friant Dam on the upper San Joaquin, operators lowered by 10 feet the dam's 18-foot drum gates. The gates are normally raised to create extra storage space. But with overflows from smaller dams upstream, operators lowered the gates to release water from the full reservoir. The outgoing flows disabled a power plant, washed out a river fish hatchery, and flooded a trailer park near Fresno.

Levees Giving Way

Up and down the waterlogged Central Valley, levees were giving way, inundating homes and fields. A 1,000-foot-wide breach flooded several small towns, claimed three lives and damaged 1,200 homes and more than 300 businesses. On the middle Sacramento, a circle of sandbagged berms saved the town of Meridian, but about 35,000 acres of farmland were flooded. Levees on the San Joaquin had ruptured in more than 30 places. The levee failures conferred a kind of mixed blessing; each time a breach opened, the water level in the main channel dropped and spared downstream communities. That, of course, was small consolation to those whose property was flooded.

It would be three days into the New Year, with the San Joaquin's tributaries still pouring huge flows into the main channel, before the radiotelemetry, the satellite messages, the inflow gauges, the USGS measurements, Rhea's orographic model and all the rest of the technology told the forecasters that the worst of the New Year's floods was over. The combination of storms had produced an average of 25 inches of rainfall across the Feather River watershed. Many rivers and reservoirs had reached record levels. Eight persons had died, nearly 300 square miles of farmland had been inundated, and an estimated 32,000 homes and businesses had been damaged or destroyed; total damages were calculated at nearly $2 billion. Yosemite National Park was closed for almost two months for repairs.

New Ways to Deal with Floods

In the wake of the floods, California began to look at new ideas for dealing with floods. Climatologists urged that the state take a closer and more global look at its long-term cycle of flood and drought. Jeffrey Mount, professor of geology at the University of California at Davis and author of *California Rivers and Streams*, publicly advocated allowing rivers to reconnect with their floodplains as a method of flood management and restricting development on flood-prone areas. Governor Pete Wilson called for increased expenditures to combat flooding and aid forecasting, including—to Mark Heggli's delight—additional telemetry for river gauges.

A Job Well Done

For the harried forecasters, flood-fighters and water management operators, it was two weeks' work to be proud of. While the timing of the rainfall occasionally eluded forecasters, the total amount forecast for the three storms was exceptionally close to what actually fell. The hydrologists came up with mostly accurate predictions not only of amounts but of timing and locations. Bowling's staff's juggling of inflows and releases had been, in Hester's words, "phenomenal" in sparing the Sacramento River and the region around it a lot more damage. The Corps of Engineers' management of reservoir flood-control space saved countless dollars of flood damage, especially in the San Joaquin Valley. Although the floods had overwhelmed or swept out several critical USGS stations, the high-tech data network had held up beautifully.

On Sunday, January 5, with the waters receding and the computer models showing dry days and clear skies ahead, Bill Mork went to church. There he met the choir member who had been so skeptical only a week before. "Well, Margaret," he said, "was that enough for you?" Sheepishly, the woman apologized for doubting him. "But please, Bill," she said, "let's don't do it again."

Restoring Wetlands to Prevent Flood Disasters

By Bob Schildgen

In the following selection Bob Schildgen describes problems created by artificial flood control methods and argues for ecological measures that can prevent disastrous floods. Schildgen says that traditional governmental methods for flood containment, which utilize levee and dam construction, have proven to be counterproductive because these structures channel and intensify river waters, actually causing floods. Billions of dollars are then spent on the rebuilding of these structures when overflowing rivers destroy them. In addition, some government agencies encourage the public to develop and live in the floodplains where rivers naturally overflow in times of flooding. Schildgen reports that many geologists advocate a move away from those practices. They recommend removing some levees, discouraging development in floodplains, and encouraging people to rebuild in safer areas after their homes have been destroyed by floods. According to Schildgen, restoring the wetlands bordering the nation's rivers would enable rivers to flood seasonally without harming people or their property. Some government agencies support these efforts, but the most progress has been made by citizens becoming involved in their own flood planning strategies and implementing more ecological solutions for their communities. Bob Schildgen is the managing editor of Sierra *magazine.*

The Deluge is ancient, universal, inevitable. Stories of a catastrophic flood were told 4,000 years ago in Mesopotamia, and have been recited from desert to rainforest, from the Natives of Australia to the Maya in Central America.

Bob Schildgen, "Unnatural Disasters," *Sierra*, vol. 84, May/June 1999, p. 48. Copyright © 1999 by The Sierra Club. Reproduced by permission.

In many of these myths, the flood is a punishment for the sins of humanity.

What sins are we suffering for now? Floods are so frequent and intense that it seems we've returned to the drenched mythic dreamtime. The trouble begins with a deep snow cover in the mountains, a quick spring thaw on the prairie, a sudden downpour, a relentless gray month of steady rain. As waters rise, people in the floodplain anxiously listen to weather reports and upstream flood measurements, and watch the muddy torrents on the news. Then comes the desperate sandbagging, pumping, bulldozing, emergency levee building. Families flee to high ground before roads and bridges wash out. Homes, farms, and businesses are ruined, submerged or ripped away in a rush of water and mud.

The human cost can be read on the faces of those huddled in makeshift shelters and school gyms, and heard in their dazed accounts of loved ones who disappeared under the waves. Our sense of what is important changes: in Grand Forks, North Dakota, a police officer boats to his ruined house, and steps out of the water into his second-story window to save his wife's wedding dress. There is heroism and sacrifice and community solidarity. One after another, survivors tell how the sundering flood made them closer than before.

Then the politicians arrive by boat and helicopter, looking grave and rugged in their flannel shirts and hunting caps and outdoor gear. The president declares a disaster, and another relief effort begins.

We call these disasters "natural" and even "acts of God." True, rivers always have and always will overflow their banks. But there is increasing evidence that human hands are roiling the already angry waters; we have forgotten the ancient lesson that floods are the price we pay for our own actions.

In an attempt to save ourselves, we build not arks, but massive dams and levees that enable us to live and farm on the lands where the water belongs. This reflexive reliance on technical fixes is notorious for ruining vital natural ecosystems. Dams obliterate river valleys, turning them into artificial lakes, while levees cut off rivers from riparian habitat. Moreover, these remedies can defeat their purpose. A growing number of flood watchers warn that excessive dependence on structures actually aggravates floods, as does our destruction of water-storing wetlands and reckless development of floodplains. We spend billions, first to prevent floods and then to recover from them, but much of that money is merely subsidizing disaster.

The U.S. Government Promotes Floodplain Development

The U.S. government does more to promote floods than any other entity. More than 40 separate federal programs and agencies, governing everything from highway construction to farm export policy, encourage building and farming on floodplains and wetlands. In 1996 alone, according to an analysis by Sierra Club Midwest representative Brett Hulsey and the National Wildlife Federation's David Conrad, over $7 billion was poured into ten programs that aggravate flooding. "So much subsidy goes into the development of floodplains that there's no incentive to stay out," says Nancy Philippi, vice president of the Wetlands Initiative in Chicago.

Between 1960 and 1985, the federal government spent $38 billion on flood control, yet average annual flood damage—adjusted for inflation—continued to increase, more than doubling. Since 1990, damages have averaged more than $5 billion a year. When rains pounded the Upper Mississippi watershed for days on end in the spring of 1993, the cost was $6.5 billion. When a "Pineapple Express" from the subtropical Pacific dumped heavy rains on California and brought on the New Year's Flood of 1997, rivers swelled and broke or overtopped many stretches of

Levee failure can result in extensive flooding. In 1927, this out-of-control steamship damaged a Louisiana levee, causing flooding in the Mississippi basin.

California's thousands of miles of levees just as they had in the Midwest—at an estimated cost of $1.7 billion. When the Red River, which flows up through the prairie between North Dakota and Minnesota, flooded later that year, another $3 billion in damages was added. The human toll is also staggering. More than 500 people have been killed since 1993 in the Great Midwest Flood and the many floods that followed, a loss that would have been far higher without modern weather forecasting and communications to spread the word to sandbag or flee.

The traditional defense against floods is to treat them as a plumbing problem. Dams are built to contain the water, and levees—mounds of earth, riprap, or concrete along the banks of the river—seek to confine it. When another 100-year flood comes ahead of schedule and washes these structures away, they are rebuilt bigger and stronger.

The bulk of the $4 billion annual budget of the U.S. Army Corps of Engineers, the federal agency primarily responsible for flood control, goes to building and maintaining waterworks. The Corps boasts that its dams and 8,500 miles of levees have saved some $387 billion in damages since 1928. No similar assessment exists of the damages wrought in areas where Corps projects encouraged development that was later inundated.

The barriers to change may be as much a matter of political culture as of the Corps' long tradition of engineering. Congress is a significant obstacle, says Larry Larson, executive director of the Association of Floodplain Managers. "They still believe all their constituents want structural solutions, because the structural cadre has been lobbying for a hundred years. Other people don't get heard from." In addition, Larson notes, there's the congressional ego factor: "Dams are 'plaqueable.' The plaque says, 'that's the senator's dam.'" Less intrusive approaches tend not to be monumental, and thus not so politically attractive.

Federal Agencies Work at Cross-Purposes

Flood management is complicated by the fact that federal agencies often work at cross-purposes. For example, while the Department of Agriculture's Wetland Reserve Program is buying up marginal cropland and restoring it as wetlands, the Corps is issuing permits that allow drainage and destruction of wetlands at the rate of 70,000 acres a year. When government-built dams and levees fail, emergency relief and federal flood insurance encourage rebuilding in the same locations. "The federal government tries to adjust nature to us, rather than letting us adjust to nature," says Larson. "It does too good a job bailing people out. If a community knows it can get a hundred percent aid to rebuild, there's no incentive for moving out." Inappropriate development in flood-prone areas occurs, he adds, because "too many city councils say, 'if we don't let them build, they'll go someplace else.' I don't blame the developers as much as city officials."

An indication of confusion as murky as the Missouri River itself comes from House Majority Leader Dick Armey. "Don't move away—rebuild," he exhorted the waterlogged folks of Grand Forks. "If I were sitting here today making that decision I'd come back." Armey's advice runs directly counter to the policies of the Federal Emergency Management Agency (FEMA), which has been trying to break the traditional flood-and-rebuild cycle by moving property out of harm's way and discouraging reckless development.

In recent years, the Corps has begun, ever so slowly, to seriously consider nonstructural approaches to flood control. It is even attempting to undo some of its past environmental damage in the Everglades and around the upper Snake River in Wyoming, where it is removing levees to let water flow into old channels.

Engineers Still Rule

Nevertheless, the engineers still rule. In California, failed levees are being rebuilt, raised, and hardened just as they are being built along the Mississippi—while other strategies are largely neglected. "Two years ago the water started to recede in California," says Jeffrey Mount, chair of the geology department at the University of California at Davis. "The reality is that despite thousands of hours of work, we're no further along than two years ago, and in many ways worse off. We remain addicted to levees as the first line of defense."

Mount advocates getting rid of some levees and moving others farther away from riverbanks, giving the river room to slow down and flow through natural paths, to loaf in sloughs and swamps and spill over into farmlands that can tolerate a certain amount of flooding. This approach would not only curb further development in these areas but also help revive much abused riparian areas.

Even when they stand firm, levees can actually cause or exacerbate floods. Constricting and intensifying the river's flow, they can channel a flood downstream, making one community's salvation another's trauma. Conversely, a breach in upstream levees can be a blessing for those downstream. During the New Year's Flood in California, says Mount, "if there had not been breaks at Olivehurst on the Feather River, it may well have flooded Sacramento."

Like California's capital, St. Louis [Missouri] may have been spared enormous damage in 1993, when the Mississippi and its tributaries topped or broke more than 1,000 upstream levees, causing vast inundations. Even so, the flood still crested in St. Louis at over 47 feet, six feet above its previous record. No one knows how much greater the destruction might have been had the levees held.

Neither the Mississippi and its tributaries' thousands of miles of levees and dozens of huge dams nor California's 6,000 miles of levees and more than 1,400 dams can reasonably be expected to do the entire job of flood control. "We cannot prevent floods," Mount warned in congressional testimony after the California flood. "The hard lesson learned is that despite our seemingly Herculean engineering efforts, floods are going to happen."

Nothing demonstrates more vividly than a river the degree to which one's own backyard is linked to the ecosystem. The Mississippi watershed, for example, drains more than one-third of the United States. A raindrop falling in Montana can end up in the Gulf of Mexico. Its destiny is determined not just by weather and the lay of the land, but by myriad human actions: agricultural tilling and drainage, suburban development, deforestation, and the decisions of hundreds of local, state, and federal agencies as well as thousands of private landowners.

Runoff from a flooded cornfield in Minnesota can end up killing fish off the coast of Louisiana, because fertilizers washed downriver promote the growth of algae that deprives the water of oxygen. (After the 1993 Mississippi flood, the zone of oxygen-depleted waters off the Louisiana coast doubled to almost 7,000 square miles.) That cornfield in the floodplain might have been planted because of agricultural subsidies, a drought in Russia, or a growing demand for bacon-burgers. A case can be made that Ronald McDonald, not nature or an angry God, is the true Lord of the Floods.

Even the amount of rain falling on the field may be tied to human activity. The recent El Niño weather system, with its increased precipitation and more intense storms, has been linked to global warming. Thus the sport utility vehicle that gets washed away in the flash flood may have helped bring about its own destruction.

A turning point in flood control came in the wake of the 1993 flood when Corps General Gerald Galloway bucked tradition and called for more emphasis on nonstructural methods, including the acquisition and restoration of wetlands and riparian habitat, stricter limits on development in floodplains, and even a farm policy that discourages the conversion of wetlands to cropland.

Wetlands can store excess water like a sponge, and in some cases may be more efficient than manmade reservoirs. Depending on the soil type, they can contain 1 million to 1.5 million gallons of water per acre, and can alleviate flooding, though no one really knows to what extent. Wetland destruction, however, clearly aggravates flooding, even on a local scale. Doris Wilson, an elementary school teacher from Louisville, explained in congressional testimony how her home flooded on March 1, 1997, because a nearby wetland had been drained by a developer. "I realize we had a lot of rain that day," she said. "However, the developer created the situation that made the flood worse."

What happened in Wilson's yard may be a miniature version of what occurs in an entire watershed. Almost 120 million acres of U.S. wetlands have been destroyed for agriculture and development, more than half of what existed prior to European conquest. California, Missouri, Iowa, and Illinois have allowed over 85 percent of their wetlands to be destroyed. Motorists rolling along midwestern highways through the vast stretches of corn and soybean fields don't realize that they're driving over the grave of a wetland, sometimes with miles of underground pipes draining off the water to prevent it from returning.

Some geologists and soil scientists consider it more than coincidence that the Red River flood occurred in an area where there has been large-scale drainage of wetlands. "Water retention is significantly less than ten, twenty, or thirty years ago," says Dexter Perkins, a geology professor at the University of North Dakota in Grand Forks. "Seventy-five percent of the wetlands in the Red River basin have been drained. In several counties it's ninety-nine percent."

Scientists Disagree

While scientists agree that wetlands can reduce flooding in upland areas, there is disagreement on whether they can prevent the flood peaks that are the major cause of damage. Donald Hey, a hydrologist with the Wetlands Initiative, contends that the excess water that poured through St. Louis in 1993 would have covered slightly more than 13 million acres—half the amount of wetlands lost in the Upper Mississippi region since 1780, but only 3 percent of the land in that area. Hey argues that "by strategically placing at least thirteen million acres of wetlands on hydric soils in the basin, we can solve the basin's flooding problems in an ecologically sound manner." The Corps' hydraulic engineers sharply dispute this analysis, saying that it would have been physically impossible for the wetlands to have contained the 1993 flood. Even if this is so, argues Perkins, the prudent course is to regard wetlands as insurance against floods, protecting and restoring what we can.

The idea that swamps and bottomlands can tame a torrent is hardly new. In 1849, Louisiana Senator Solomon Downs testified on the Swamp Act, which transferred federally owned wetlands to the states and opened them up to development. "It is reasonable to suppose that the whole country is now more rapidly and thoroughly drained into the Mississippi than when in a state of nature," Downs said. "Then, no doubt, a great quantity of water was collected in pools and swamps, and there remained until carried off by gradual evaporation." The issue of flood control on the river was hotly debated for years after the Swamp Act began to bring massive new settlement on the floodplains, with one camp in favor of levees and the other for backing off from the river. The levee advocates won out, but the most massive federal projects on the Mississippi were not undertaken until after the flood of 1927. Gilbert F. White, generally acknowledged as the nation's foremost authority on floods, was already making a case for nonstructural methods in the 1930s, when he served as an advisor to President Franklin D. Roosevelt's administration.

Once the waters recede, the debris has been hauled away (100 tons a day in Grand Forks in 1997), and rebuilding begins, people tend to leave flood control to community leaders and the federal government. Making public policy is tedious enough in good times, let alone when a family is confronted with a houseful of mud, molding wallboard, and wrecked appliances. "Our flood memory half-life is remarkably short," says Galloway. One victim of the Red River flood told Minnesota Public Radio that her home was in the 500 year floodplain, "so I figure I won't see another flood like this 'cause I won't live that long."

More and more Americans are living in harm's way: FEMA has identified 10 million households and businesses with property valued at a trillion dollars on some 150,000 square miles in flood-prone areas. Cities and towns grew up on rivers because of the need for inland water transport, and once established they cannot very well pack up and move. But ceasing to build on the most vulnerable areas would clearly reduce the damage and loss of life. And while the rich alluvial soil of floodplains makes fine farmland, not every acre has to be cultivated right to the edge of a river.

Communities Change Their Flood Control Plans

Increasingly, communities are opting out of the flood-and-rebuild cycle. After a 1972 flood killed 238 people and caused $500 million in damages, Rapid City, South Dakota, used federal funds to buy 1,400 pieces of property and create a greenway. After the town of Valmeyer, Illinois, was flooded in 1993, 600 residents used $35 million in state and federal aid to move to higher ground. In St. Charles County, Missouri, a similar relocation after the 1993 flood meant that when the river flooded again in 1995, damage and the cost of disaster relief was a fraction of the previous total. Soldiers Grove, Wisconsin, has avoided disaster by moving its business district away from the Kickapoo River and creating a new town center. And in Napa, California, where flooding costs have averaged $15 million a year since 1960, citizens rejected a plan by the Army Corps to dredge the Napa River and build more levees. Instead, a broad coalition campaigning on the slogan "a living river" mustered the necessary two-thirds vote last year to restore 600 acres of marshland, move levees back from the river, and relocate more than 60 structures off the floodplain.

Tulsa, Oklahoma, has gone from almost total reliance on structural control to a more integrated approach. In 1964, after the Corps of Engineers completed the Keystone Dam 15 miles upstream, Tulsa believed it was finally secure from the constant flooding of the Arkansas River. Lowland meadows were paved over and developed, and the population grew by 25 percent in the 1960s. When flooding did occur, the response was the typical return and rebuild—until the 1976 Memorial Day Flood that took three lives and wrought $40 million in damages. Tulsa citizens recognized that it might have been worse if a large local park had not been preserved as open space. So after the deluge, Tulsans elected new city commissioners who declared a moratorium on floodplain construction. After a second Memorial Day Flood killed 14 people and caused $180 million in damage in 1984, Tulsans pushed the nonstructural solution further. Working with FEMA, the city relocated over 500 houses and mobile homes and ultimately moved more than 900 buildings out of the most critical areas.

In most of these situations, local citizens broke the pattern of leaving things to the experts and became deeply involved in the planning themselves. Larson of the Association of Floodplain Managers emphasizes the importance of citizen participation in developing a comprehensive plan that takes into account the entire local economy. Local citizens are also needed to change attitudes in Congress, and with more people involved, it is easier for municipalities to thread through the various bureaucracies to find and secure state and federal aid.

FEMA Helps Out

In the states affected by the Midwest floods, FEMA has helped buy out or relocate more than 20,000 properties at a cost of only $480 million—a bargain in that every dollar spent saves two on future disaster relief costs—and the agency would like to acquire more. "We have identified 35,000 repetitive flood-loss properties across the country that have had two or more flood-loss claims in the past ten years," says FEMA director Tames Lee Witt. The agency hoped to relocate 7,300 of these properties, which would cost $300 million over a three-year period, but ultimately save an estimated $1 billion in damages. Under the Clinton administration's . . . budget, however, FEMA expects an $88 million shortfall for these programs.

Unfortunately, the disaster policy mandated by Congress remains backward, treating symptoms rather than causes and shelling out more money for disaster relief than for prevention. (For example, FEMA is allowed to use only 15 percent of the total spent on disaster relief for mitigation.) Thus Witt is proposing other measures to discourage building and living in the danger zone, such as refusing to issue flood insurance to property owners who have filed two or more flood claims.

Another important effort is the Agriculture Department's Wetlands Reserve Program, which has set aside 665,000 acres of

wetlands.... The cost of restoration overall averages about $200
per acre; in some places the wetland can return simply by being
left alone, while in others considerable work is required to re-
contour and revegetate the landscape. The program usually pur-
chases a perpetual easement to the land at prices based on its
value as agricultural land. "This totally changed the land use on
marginal lands," says Wetlands Reserve Program Director Bob
Misso. "It's a hell of a deal for taxpayers, for landowners, and for
the environment." Since the acquisition cost is often capped at
$800 an acre, however, and the price is pegged to agricultural
value, the program doesn't work when speculative developers
have driven up land prices. And some farmers consider the com-
pensation inadequate. In North Dakota, only three square miles
has been enrolled in the program.

Although there are many mysteries in the soul of a river and
the heart of a flood, it is becoming clear that we all would benefit from a remedy that environmentalists have long pleaded for:
reducing human impact on the earth by protecting and restoring
natural places, building compactly and halting sprawl, and curb-
ing population growth. The other thing we have learned about
flood prevention is the oldest truism of democracy, that active
engagement by a broad, well-informed citizenry is key to im-
proving the way things are done.

No matter what we do, catastrophic rains will fall and im-
placable torrents will flow, and we will never control them completely. But with a combination of respect for nature and re-
straint in our own actions, we stand a better chance of riding
out the storm.

Using New Technologies to Improve Flood Warning Systems

By David Ford, Dudley McFadden,
and Marsha Hilmes-Robinson

Because floods come and go quickly, cities cannot monitor flooding by simply watching water levels rise but must implement a flood warning system to anticipate the floods and predict the extent of possible flood damages. To realize this goal, Fort Collins, Colorado, is using tools once reserved for federal agencies, such as digital technology, to improve the city's flood forecasting system. Digital technology automatically processes flood information, which improves flood monitoring and allows more rapid notification of emergency responders to the threat of flooding. In combination with other new technologies, digital technology saves Fort Collins money and lives.

David Ford is the president of David Ford Consulting Engineers of Sacramento, California, and Dudley McFadden is a project engineer at the firm. Marsha Hilmes-Robinson is the floodplain administrator for the city of Fort Collins.

T hanks to recent improvements in digital technology, the city of Fort Collins, Colorado, now has a warning system that can accurately predict the location and severity of an impending flood.

Following a 30-hour rain event in 1997 that culminated with a downpour on July 28, a devastating flash flood occurred in Fort Collins, Colorado, a city of approximately 119,000 located 50

David Ford, Dudley McFadden, and Marsha Hilmes-Robinson, "Early Warning," *Civil Engineering*, vol. 72, August 2002, p. 62. Copyright © 2002 by *Civil Engineering*. Reproduced by permission.

miles (80 km) north of Denver. The storm—one of the biggest ever documented in an urban area in the state—set records for three-hour and six-hour precipitation totals in Fort Collins. The resulting flood killed five people and caused more than $200 million in property damage.

Although severe, the damage could have been much worse. In the years before the flood, Fort Collins had prepared for such an event by carrying out drainage and storm-water management projects, acquiring and moving structures from high-risk areas, and implementing an aggressive floodplain management program designed to reduce risks through judicious development in flood-prone areas. Some credit these actions with saving nearly 100 lives and reducing the damage in the 1997 flood by as much as $5 million.

However, the flood proved that more work needed to be done. After it was over, Fort Collins set out to refine its flood warning system, regarding it as an important part of the overall solution to the flooding problem. City staff members realized that improvements to the system could give emergency responders and citizens more warning of impending floods. With even a few additional minutes of lead time, emergency managers could anticipate hazards and respond more efficiently, and citizens would be in a better position to move property—and themselves—out of harm's way.

The Importance of Digital Technology

Digital technology figures prominently in flood warning systems. Not only does the technology improve the monitoring and managing of rainfall and water level data; it also lends itself to mathematical models for forecasting water levels. Digital technology automatically compares forecast and observed conditions with predefined thresholds, rapidly notifying emergency responders of flood threats and providing them with inundation information not otherwise available. Armed with this information, emergency response personnel may not be able to prevent a flood, but they can do more to reduce the damage it causes.

The goal of the Fort Collins flood warning system is to marshal information, equipment, personnel, and procedures in such a way as to protect people and property to the fullest extent possible. The process begins with data collection and transmission. An automated rainfall and water level gauging system gathers and sends the data via radio to a base station, where the information is filed, displayed, and evaluated. The evaluation includes examining the rainfall and water level reports to spot current threats and predicting levels so as to discern future threats. If a threat is detected, emergency personnel are notified and the response begins. The response includes such measures as evacuating people at risk, controlling traffic, implementing temporary floodproofing measures, and providing backups for vital services. A detailed flood response plan—a component of Fort Collins's emergency operations plan—spells out the procedures for these actions.

ALERT Technology

The data collection and transmission system owned and operated by the city uses off-the-shelf automated local evaluation in real time (ALERT) technology. Developed in the 1970s by the National Weather Service, ALERT technology relies on remote sensors in the field to collect environmental data and route them to a central location. The sensors continuously measure rainfall, water level, and other hydrometeorological factors. Data are transmitted from the gauge whenever conditions change by a predetermined amount.

For example, the Fort Collins flood warning system uses tipping-bucket rain gauges, which collect rainfall and direct it into one of two small buckets on the gauge. With each 0.04 inch (1 mm) of rainfall, each bucket becomes filled to capacity and tips through gravity. The movement closes an electric circuit, which causes a radio at the monitoring site to transmit the measurement. Similar configurations are used for sensing and transmitting water level, wind speed, and other important environmental conditions.

The city employs 44 gauges as part of its flood warning system: 6 are complete weather stations, 12 measure precipitation only, 9 measure water levels only, and 17 measure precipitation and water levels. To determine which streams were to be monitored by the gauges, staff members reviewed the location of vulnerable property and examined historical records. For example, streams with a history of overflowing and damaging property in the urban area are monitored, while those in agricultural areas are not. To maximize warning time, the gauges were positioned upstream of the areas considered to be at risk.

In Fort Collins, rain gauges are installed at the top of standpipes, which are open. A water level sensor is placed in a stream and connected via an electrical conduit to the radio transmitter, which resides in a watertight enclosure inside the standpipe. The transmitter's antenna is mounted to the side of the standpipe, and a solar panel charges the battery for the sensors and transmitter.

Signals from the gauges are sent to one of the city's two base stations, each of which houses a computer with a radio receiver and an encoder—an electronic device that extracts the signal from the radio wave and converts it to digital input. The engineering quantity represented by the inputs is then stored in a computer database. Fort Collins uses an off-the-shelf environmental data management and display application called DIADvisor, which is manufactured by DIAD, Inc., of Longmont, Colorado. The program provides city staff with a map of the entire city and surrounding area and includes a color-coded overlay to indicate the location and intensity of rainfall. This "rainfall field" is the first of several visualization tools that come into play in evaluating a flood threat.

Using the WatchDog

To supplement the flood detection capabilities provided by DIADvisor, the city implemented an automated threat detection system with the assistance of David Ford Consulting Engineers, a civil engineering firm based in Sacramento, California. This decision support system, known as WatchDog, works much like the antivirus software on a computer: It runs continuously, inspecting in real time the incoming data as they are stored in the DIADvisor database, comparing the rainfall and water level observations with thresholds specified by city staff, and notifying the user of any threatening conditions. Staff members determine the thresholds based upon their knowledge of the capacity of particular waterways and the location and elevation of vulnerable property. For example, staff members know that if the water depth at the gauge on Fossil Creek at College Avenue reaches 12.7 ft (3.9 m), overtopping of College Avenue will begin. Thus, if the observed water level reaches 11.7 ft (3.6 m) and continues rising, action will be taken. When WatchDog determines that a threshold has been exceeded, it notifies staff and emergency responders by sending e-mails, faxes, or pages.

Despite the usefulness of the ALERT gauges and the decision support system, city staff realized that these tools by themselves would not increase the warning time to the extent they desired. In Fort Collins, the floods come and go quickly. Simply waiting for the water levels to rise was not an adequate way to detect a threat—forecasting the rise would be better. To provide as much warning as possible, the staff needed to be able to anticipate flooding and predict the extent to which it could affect land, structures, roads, and other property.

A Software System to Forecast Water Levels

To attain that capability, the city commissioned David Ford Consulting Engineers to develop a water level forecasting tool that would predict water levels based on current rainfall observations and rainfall forecasts. The task required addressing four major challenges: First, the city wanted something easy to use, maintain, and expand; second, it needed a system that would act rapidly—too slow meant too late. The third challenge was to incorporate the watershed and channel modeling that had been implemented in previous storm-water management studies. Finally, the forecasting system had to lend itself to full integration into the city's existing gauging system and other information systems available to the city.

To meet the city's needs, the consultant created a software system that incorporates Fort Collins's existing watershed and channel models. To predict runoff patterns in the local watershed, city engineers use the U.S. Environmental Protection Agency's Storm Water Management Model (SWMM), a comprehensive computer program used to simulate rainfall runoff. For channel modeling, city staff members rely on software developed by the U.S. Army Corps of Engineers' Hydrologic Engineering Center (HEC), namely HEC-2 (Water Surface Profiles) and HEC-RAS (River Analysis System). These programs were incorporated into a forecasting framework in a way that required little modification of existing models, and members of the staff can now easily use, upgrade, and maintain the system. . . .

Storm-water specialists and floodplain managers in Fort Collins can review the SWMM, HEC-2, and HEC-RAS reports to determine sites and facilities that are vulnerable to flooding. These employees, in turn, can notify emergency responders and interpret the results for them. However, staff members who are not flood specialists—especially the city's emergency responders—wanted to receive the information in a more comprehensible format. As a first step toward meeting this need, software was developed to read the reports created by SWMM, HEC-2, and HEC-RAS. The results—computed flow rates and depths of flow in channels and in the adjacent floodplain—are then presented as charts and graphs in a graphical interface.

Using the Geographic Information System

To enhance the readability of the information, inundation maps were created to illustrate which surfaces in a given area are likely to be flooded and which are expected to remain above the floodwaters. To fashion these maps, another tool of digital technology—a geographic information system (GIS)—was used. The city has previously commissioned a high-resolution survey of terrain in Fort Collins. Because the GIS spatial analysis tools are linked to the HEC-2 and HEC-RAS models, the elevation data from that earlier survey can be used to generate inundation maps "on the fly" as the water level forecasts are made. As each forecast is completed, the inundation maps are created by further processing the results of the water surface elevation computations made by HEC-2 or HEC-RAS. Given channel geometry and a steady flow rate—the peak forecast flow from SWMM—both programs compute the elevation at stream cross sections.

After the water surface elevations are computed, GIS tools are used to create a set of planes that represent the water surface between adjacent cross sections. With the GIS tools, these planes are intersected mathematically with planes that represent the ground surface and objects on the ground. If the ground surface elevation is less than the elevation of the water surface plane, it will be inundated and thus not visible on the map. Otherwise, the ground will not be inundated and will be visible.

By itself, the resulting image provides useful information for emergency response personnel. However, the inundation map can also be combined with an aerial photograph of the area at risk of flooding, giving emergency responders an even more helpful and easily interpreted image. For example, shading can be superimposed on an aerial photograph to represent the forecast flood depth and illustrate precisely where the flooding is expected to occur. In this way, emergency responders can quickly distinguish structures at risk, roads that should be closed or avoided, and other "hot spots" in need of attention.

To ensure that the inundation maps are available to those who need them for response, the Fort Collins flood warning system stores the digital maps on a server on the city's high-speed local area network. All response personnel can then connect to that server, retrieve the map, and view it with software on their own computer at virtually any location.

The Cost of the System

On average, the total capital cost for each rainfall and water level gauge, with installation, was approximately $7,000. The total cost of the data collection and transmission system, including the data management software, radio repeaters, and related items, was about $450,000. The decision support system cost approximately $250,000 to develop and implement, not including the cost to create the detailed terrain data in the GIS. Part of the funding for the flood warning system was provided by a grant from the Federal Emergency Management Agency (FEMA). Now that the city's flood warning system has been implemented, the only significant operational expense is the labor cost: One city employee works full time with the gauge network and the software, and other staff members work with the decision support system as needed.

Because of the flood warning system, Fort Collins has enjoyed cost savings through reduced flood insurance premiums. The national flood insurance program administered by FEMA assigns participating communities a rating that is based upon their efforts to reduce flood risk, a higher score yielding lower flood insurance premiums. Partly because of its flood warning system, Fort Collins has one of the best ratings. However, the city feels that the system's benefits extend beyond the economic realm—if even one life is saved, it will have been worth the cost.

Recent advances in digital technology have made the Fort Collins flood warning system possible. Just a few years ago, only federal agencies such as the National Weather Service and the U.S. Army Corps of Engineers had access to the technology necessary for real-time threat recognition, namely workstations, real-time hydrometeorological data, detailed terrain data, powerful watershed and channel models, and GIS tools. Fortunately, these tools are now more readily available and can be used on the pc-based system owned and operated by Fort Collins. Of course, the

National Weather Service and other federal agencies still play an important role in flood response efforts in Fort Collins. However, by providing additional information tailored to local conditions and designed for optimal use by emergency personnel, the flood warning system enables the city to mount a rapid and focused response to potentially damaging and life-threatening floods.

Major River Floods Worldwide

Date	Country	River	Casualties
1824	Russia	Neva	10,000
1887	China	Huang He	1 million
1913	USA	Ohio	500
1931	China	Yangtze	1 million
1933	China	Huang He	3 million
1938	China	Huang He	3–4 million
1948	China	Min	3,500
1954	China	Yangtze	30,000
1988	Bangladesh	Ganges and Brahmaputra	1,000
1993	USA	Mississippi	48
1997	USA	Red	Unknown

Dougal Dixon, *Natural Disasters*. London: Reader's Digest, 1997.

GLOSSARY

acre-foot: The amount of water required to cover one acre to a depth of one foot. An acre-foot equals 326,851 gallons or 43,560 cubic feet.

annual flood: The maximum discharge peak during a given water year (October 1–September 30).

backflow: The backing up of water through a conduit or channel in the direction opposite of normal flow.

bank: The margins of a channel. Banks are called right or left as viewed facing in the direction of the flow.

base flood: The national standard for floodplain management is the base, or 1 percent chance flood. This flood has at least one chance in one hundred of occurring in any given year. It is also called a hundred-year flood.

basin: An area having a common outlet for its surface runoff.

cfs (cubic feet per second): The flow rate or discharge equal to one cubic foot (of water, usually) per second. This rate is equivalent to approximately 7.48 gallons per second. This is also referred to as a second-foot.

channel (watercourse): An open conduit either naturally or artificially created which periodically, or continuously contains moving water, or forms a connection link between two bodies of water. River, creek, run, branch, anabranch, and tributary are some of the terms used to describe natural channels. Natural channels may be single or braided. Canal and floodway are some of the terms used to describe artificial channels.

channelizaton: The modification of a natural river channel; may include deepening, widening, or straightening.

crest: The highest stage or level of a flood wave as it passes a point. Also, the top of a dam, dike, spillway, or weir, to which water must rise before passing over the structure.

dam: Any artificial barrier which impounds or diverts water. The dam is generally hydrologically significant if it is twenty-five feet or more in height from the natural bed of the stream and has a storage of at least fifteen acre-feet or has an impounding capacity of fifty acre-feet or more and is at least six feet above the natural bed of the stream.

dam failure: A catastrophic event characterized by the sudden, rapid, and uncontrolled release of impounded water.

dike: The term used to describe an embankment that blocks an area on a reservoir or lake rim that is lower than the top of the dam.

direct flood damage: The damage done to property, structures, and goods by a flood, as measured by the cost of replacement and repairs.

discharge: The rate at which water passes a given point. Discharge is another term for streamflow and is usually expressed in cubic feet per second.

diversion: The taking of water from a stream or other body of water into a canal, pipe, or other conduit.

drainage basin: A part of the surface of the earth that is occupied by a drainage system, which consists of a surface stream or a body of impounded surface water together with all tributary surface streams and bodies of impounded surface water.

flash flood: A flood which flows within a few hours (usually less than six hours) of heavy or excessive rainfall, dam or levee failure, or the sudden release of water impounded by an ice jam.

flash flood warning (FFW): A warning by the National Weather Service issued to inform that flash flooding is imminent or occurring.

flash flood watch (FFA): A statement by the National Weather Service that alerts communities to the possibility of flash flooding in specific areas.

flood: The inundation of a normally dry area caused by high flow or overflow of water in an established watercourse, such as a river, stream, or drainage ditch.

flood crest: The maximum height of a flood wave as it passes a location.

floodplain: The relatively flat lowland that borders a river, usually dry but subject to flooding. Floodplain soils actually are former flood deposits.

flood warning (FLW): A release by the National Weather Service to inform the public of flooding along larger streams in which there is a serious threat to life or property.

hydrograph: A graph that shows changes in discharge or river stage over time. The time scale may be in minutes, hours, days, months, years, or decades.

hydrology: The science dealing with the properties, distribution, and circulation of water on the earth's surface, below the ground, and in the atmosphere.

ice jam: A stationary accumulation of ice that restricts or blocks streamflow.

levee: A long, narrow embankment usually built to protect land from flooding. If built of concrete or masonry, the structure is usually referred to as a floodwall. Levees and floodwalls confine streamflow within a specified area to prevent flooding.

major flooding: A general term used to describe floods that cause extensive inundation and property damage. (Usually characterized by the evacuation of people and livestock and the closure of both primary and secondary roads.)

minor flooding: A general term used to describe floods that cause minimal or no property damage but possibly some public inconvenience.

moderate flooding: The inundation of secondary roads where transfer to higher elevation is necessary to save property; some evacuation may be required.

peak discharge: The rate of discharge of a volume of water passing a given location (usually in cubic feet per second).

ponding: A term used to denote what happens in flat areas, when runoff collects in depressions and cannot drain out.

precipitation: As used in hydrology, precipitation is the discharge of water in a liquid or solid state, out of the atmosphere, generally onto a land or water surface. The term is commonly used to designate the quantity of water that is precipitated. Precipitation includes rainfall, snow, hail, and sleet, and is therefore a more general term than rainfall.

recurrence interval or return period: The average number of years between floods of a certain size. The actual number of years between floods of any given size varies because of the naturally changing climate.

reservoir: A man-made facility for the storage, regulation, and controlled release of water.

riparian zone: A stream and all the vegetation on its banks.

river basin: The drainage area of a river and its tributaries.

river flooding: The rise of a river to an elevation such that the river overflows its natural banks, causing or threatening damage.

river gauge: A device for measuring the river stage.

river stage: The height of the water in the river, measured relative to an arbitrary fixed point.

river system: All of the streams and channels draining a river basin.

runoff: That part of precipitation that flows toward streams on the surface of the ground or within the ground. Runoff is composed of baseflow and surface runoff.

soil moisture: Water that is contained in the upper regions near the earth's surface.

streamflow: Water that is flowing in the stream channel. The term is often used interchangeably with discharge.

surface runoff: The runoff that travels overland to the stream channel. Rain that falls on the stream channel is often combined with this quantity.

surface water: Water that flows in streams, rivers, natural lakes, wetlands, and in reservoirs constructed by humans.

tipping-bucket rain gauge: A precipitation gauge where collected water is funneled into a two-compartment bucket; a quantity of rain will fill one compartment and overbalance the bucket so that it tips, emptying into a reservoir and moving the second compartment into place beneath the funnel. As the bucket is tipped, it actuates an electric circuit.

watershed or drainage basin: The land area from which water drains toward a common watercourse on a natural basin.

wetlands: These are transitional areas between open water and dry land where the water may not be on the surface at all times, making it hard to recognize. Wetlands are generally extremely valuable and productive ecosystems.

FOR FURTHER RESEARCH

Books

John M. Barry, *Rising Tide: The Great Mississippi Flood of 1927 and How It Changed America.* New York: Simon & Schuster, 1997.

Stanley A. Changnon, ed., *The Great Flood of 1993: Causes, Impacts, and Responses.* Boulder, CO: Westview Press, 1996.

David Chapman, *Natural Hazards.* Melbourne, Australia: Oxford University Press, 1994.

Pete Daniel, *Deep'n as It Come: The 1927 Mississippi River Flood.* New York: Oxford University Press, 1977.

Dugal Dixon, *Natural Disasters.* London: Reader's Digest Association, 1997.

Kai T. Erikson, *Everything in Its Path: Destruction of Community in the Buffalo Creek Flood.* New York: Simon & Schuster, 1976.

Brian M. Fagan, *Floods, Famines, and Emperors: El Niño and the Fate of Civilizations.* New York: Basic Books, 1999.

Willis Fletcher Johnson, *The Johnstown Flood.* Philadelphia: Edgewood Publishing, 1889.

Brian J. Knapp, *Flood.* Austin, TX: Steck-Vaughn, 1990.

Patricia Lauber, *Flood: Wrestling with the Mississippi.* Washington, DC: National Geographic Society, 1996.

Luna B. Leopold, *Waters, Rivers and Creeks.* Sausalito, CA: University Science Books, 1997.

David McCullough, *The Johnstown Flood: The Incredible Story Behind One of the Most Devastating "Natural" Disasters America Has Ever Known.* New York: Simon & Schuster, 1968.

National Research Council, *A Safer Future: Reducing the Impacts of Natural Disasters.* Washington, DC: National Academy Press, 1991.

Lesley Newson, *Devastation! The World's Worst Natural Disasters.* New York: DK Publishing, 1998.

Alice Outwater, *Water: A Natural History.* New York: BasicBooks, 1996.

David Roland, ed., *Nature on the Rampage.* Washington, DC: Smithsonian, 1994.

Ted Steinberg, *Acts of God.* New York: Oxford University Press, 2000.

Periodicals

William H. Allen, "The Great Flood of 1993," *Bioscience*, December 1993.

Patricia Barnes-Svarney, "Awful Agnes," *Weatherwise*, May 2002.

Dennis L. Breo, "Flood, Sweat, and Tears—Trying to Build 'Emotional Levees,'" *JAMA*, December 1993.

Barry Came and Jake MacDonald, "Canada Mopping Up: Manitobans Face the Hard Part as the Flood Recedes," *Maclean's*, May 1997.

Craig Childs, "Haunted Canyon: Flash Floods in the Grand Canyon," *Backpacker*, May 2000.

Economist, "Bangladesh in Troubled Waters," May 11, 1991.

Mark Fischetti, "Drowning New Orleans," *Scientific American*, October 2001.

Thomas Hayden, "From Fire to Floods," *Newsweek*, October 2000.

Robert Henson, "Up to Our Necks," *Weatherwise*, March/April 1998.

David H. Hickcox, "And Then the Rains Came," *Focus*, Summer 1993.

Shahreen Kamaluddin, "Treading Water," *Far Eastern Economic Review*, December 31, 1998.

Richard A. Kerr, "A Victim of the Black Sea Flood Found," *Science*, September 2000.

Robert Kunzig, "Turning the Tide," *U.S. News & World Report*, October 2002.

Terry Martin, "Up a Raging River Without a Paddle," *Europe*, November 2002.

National Wildlife, "Seeking an End to a Flood of Claims," June/July 1999.

Public Works, "South Florida Uses GIS to Prepare for Floods," April 2002.

Jim Reed, "Against the River," *Weatherwise*, October/November 1993.

John Tibbetts, "Waterproofing the Midwest," *Planning*, April 1994.

Linda Tischler, "Grand Forks and East Grand Forks: After the Flood," *Fast Company*, June 2002.

James T. B. Tripp, "Flooding: Who Is to Blame?" *USA Today*, July 1994.

Diane Turbide, "Canada: I've Cried Two Rivers: Manitobans Struggle to Rebuild After the Flood," *Maclean's*, October 1997.

Jack Williams, "The Great Flood," *Weatherwise*, February/March 1994.

Rae Zimmerman and Robert J. Coontz Jr., "After the Deluge," *Sciences*, July/August 1994.

Websites

American Red Cross, www.redcross.org. This site features information on floods and flood preparedness, how to reduce potential flood damage, and what to do when flood warnings are issued.

Corps of Engineers, www.usace.army.mil. This website has extensive information on floods, flood-proofing, and many on-line pamphlets.

Dartmouth Flood Observatory, www.dartmouth.edu. This website provides yearly catalogs, maps, and images of river floods from 1985 to the present. It has an active archive of large flood events, and current information on flooding and using satellite technology.

FEMA, www.fema.gov. The Federal Emergency Management Agency site provides key phone numbers, flood preparedness and recovery information, flood news from individual states, maps, and weather links.

Floods, www.colorado.edu. This site provides an index of links to many flood sites.

InFocus-Flood!, www.pbs.org. This is a website for students featuring real-life flood accounts, scientific flood information, stories of flood fighters, and links to additional resources.

NOAA Home Page-Floods, www.noaa.gov. The National Oceanic and Atmospheric Administration hosts this website which provides current information on floods, flash floods, safety rules, flash flood tip sheets, and other links. Their hydrologic information center features a map showing current river conditions in the United States.

NOVA Flood!,www.pbs.org. This website has information about the Great Mississippi/Missouri Flood of 1993 as well as an audio link to "hear the flood," water graphics, and a transcript of the television broadcast, "Flood!"

The SAST Database, http://edc.usgs.gov. The Scientific Assessment and Strategy Team provides an in-depth scientific approach to flood research. This site offers data and images presented from studies done on the Mississippi and Missouri River basins, before, during, and after floods, as well as socioeconomic aspects of flooding in the United States.

USGS Water Resources Information, http://water.usgs.gov. The U.S. Geological Survey offers real-time hydrologic data, up-to-date satellite imagery, reports, and many fact sheets.